GRASS

GRASS

The Everything, Everywhere Plant

by AUGUSTA GOLDIN

publishers since 1798

THOMAS NELSON INC., PUBLISHERS

Nashville   New York

First edition

Library of Congress Cataloging in Publication Data

Goldin, Augusta R
  Grass: The Everything, Everywhere Plant.

  Bibliography: p.
  SUMMARY: Describes the characteristics and uses of various types of grass
including oats, barley, and wheat with a discussion of their importance to human
and animal life.
    1. Grasses—Juvenile literature. [1. Grasses] I. Title.
QK495.G74G64   584'.9   76–52502
ISBN 0–8407–6453–7

Acknowledgments

I am grateful to the experts in the field who read the manuscript and contributed suggestions and criticisms: Chester F. Bellard, State Conservationist of Mississippi; Jerome Hytry, State Conservationist of Wisconsin; Katherine Mergen, Head, Educational Relations, Information Division, the Soil Conservation Service, Washington, D.C.; Norman Michie, Information Liaison Officer, Food and Agricultural Organization, the United Nations, N.Y.C.; and Dr. John Tedrow, Professor of Soils, Rutgers University, New Brunswick, N.J.

Sincere appreciation for exciting and up-to-the-minute literature is also extended to: Dr. J.C. Torio, Head of the Information Services of the International Rice Research Institute, Manila, Philippines; Stephen M. Polcin, Advertising Production Manager of the Jacobsen Manufacturing Company, Racine, Wisconsin; and Jim Wilson of the Wilson Seed Farms, Polk, Nebraska.

And special thanks are due to Dr. Milton A. Sprague, Professor of Plant Morphology, Rutgers University, for his assistance and warm, directional encouragement.

Contents

To
Milton Alan Sprague

Grass is the forgiveness of nature . . . her constant benediction. . . . Should its harvest fail for a single year, famine would depopulate the world.

John James Ingalls, U.S. Senator from Kansas, 1873–1891

CHAPTER 1

Grass Is Nature's Benediction

Grass is nature's benediction. Prairies, blackened by fire, grow green with the coming of spring. Gardens, untended, are obliterated by tall grasses. And sidewalks, abandoned by walking feet, are soon carpeted with crabgrass and fescue, Bermuda grass or creeping bent.

Grass seeds are carried by the wind and running waters, by wandering animals and flying birds. Falling on meadows and mountains and swamps, on deserts and roads and rooftops, many of these grass seeds sprout and begin to grow. Grass plants grow almost everywhere, and they grow so abundantly, they wrap the earth in an emerald haze.

The great grass family, called Gramineae, includes thousands of wild and cultivated grasses for nearly every climate and every terrain. Grass grows beyond the Arctic Circle, chilled by the polar winds. It flourishes in the hot tropics, watered by torrential rains. It thrives under the temperate sun. It struggles in the desert and on the shores of salty seas.

One grass differs from another. Near the poles and on

some lofty mountaintops, grass grows crisp and short, a quarter inch, no more. In the tropics, bamboos reach upward a hundred feet or more, on stems that may be three feet around. So tough, so durable is bamboo grass that Oriental peasants often build their houses of it. Boatbuilders make unsinkable rafts of bamboo poles and tall masts for ships. On these, they transport the bamboo articles they fashion for sale—boxes and baskets and furniture, fancy walking sticks, and long, hollow poles that will be used as water pipes, and as supports for children's "hanging gardens" in countries such as India.

Some grasses are prized for their utility. Others combine utility with beauty as they green lawns and parks and golf courses. Still others provide food, sustaining us with bread and cereals and sugar. In the fields, sod grasses provide forage for grazing animals—the wild ones as well as the domesticated ones that yield milk and meat for the table.

On Planet Earth, wherever the grasses grow, they cover the soil and hold it in place. In summer, they prevent it from drying out and blowing away in clouds of dust. In spring, their matted roots, soaking up rainfall and snow-melt, prevent the thundering rush of floodwaters and the silent slippage of hillside mud.

Of all the plants in the world, the grasses are the most important to the life of the planet, because by protecting the soil, they keep it from eroding. In turn, the protected soil supports the growing grass. And grass is food for man and beast.

According to the Bible, it was on the third day of Creation that God said, "Let the Earth bring forth grass. . . ." (Gen. 1:11). Millennia later, He said, "I will send grass in thy fields for thy cattle, that thou mayest eat and be full." (Deut. 11:15.) Still later, the Hebrew prophets counseled, "All flesh is grass" (Isa. 40:6), using this universally necessary plant as the symbol of the brevity of life.

Paleontologists, scientists who deal with the life of the past, estimate that, seventy million years ago, the seeds of primitive grasses nourished the tiny, furry, four-footed mammals that scampered between the feet of the dinosaurs. The mighty dinosaurs, it is believed, died out be-

Volkswagen stationed in front of the feathery bamboos to show contrast in height.
Courtesy IRRI, Philippines

cause the climate grew colder and their food supply of towering swamp plants vanished. But the tiny mammals, sustained by grass seeds, thrived and multiplied in the changing environment.

The grasses growing at Los Banos in the Philippines—rice in the paddy, backed by a cornfield, which is backed by a stand of bamboo.   *United Nations photo*

From the beginning of history, the human family has also been sustained by the seeds of wild grasses. Ancient, well-preserved seeds have been recovered from the internal organs of Iron Age corpses, buried in Danish peat bogs. They have also been recovered from massive mammoths, frozen in Siberian ice. Impressions of grain seeds have been found on prehistoric handmade pots in Scandinavia. Grass seeds, carbonized like charcoal, have been unearthed by archaeologists near old hearths and parching ovens. Mummified seeds of millet and barley were discovered in the stomachs of mummies in an Egyptian cemetery, dating back five thousand years. And digs at the Swiss Lake settlements have uncovered seeds of wheat, millet, and barley.

So the centuries passed. Gradually, the human families

Bamboo poles support the children's "hanging garden" in Orissa, India.
United Nations photo.

stopped relying on the hunt to supplement their diet of seeds and fruit. They became herders of cattle and growers of grain. With the changing seasons, some wandered from green valleys to upland meadows, to the high, grassy plateaus of summer. Always the wandering took them to newer, lusher pastures. There, freshened by wind and beating raindrops, the good grass was converted into good flesh on the grazing cows and goats and sheep. And all this time, the children gathered the seeds of wild wheat and rye and oats, their elders baked the seeds into rough, unleavened bread, and the leftover seeds of barley and millet and sorghum were crushed for the porridge bowls.

Then, after a while, man learned to sow those wild seeds of grass. Many families stopped wandering and settled in small villages. In summer, they grazed their herds on communal grasslands. In winter, they fed them the wild and cultivated grasses, which had been cut and stored.

On occasion, when grasslands were overgrazed, the villagers moved themselves and their cattle to more distant areas. The quest was always the same—green grass for the animals, and grass seeds for themselves. In this way, they provided themselves with bread and meat.

In time, the villages became cities, and the city people, with little access to the fields, became dependent on the farmers for their food.

In the nineteenth century, during the industrial Revolution, thousands of laborers were drawn to the city factories, away from the green fields. Then the production of cereal grasses for man and forage grasses for cattle took on a new importance. By the twentieth century, as the cities grew larger, the production of grain and livestock became big business.

By the middle of the twentieth century, the production of grass had become everybody's business. Medical research had so successfully increased the life span of people that hundreds of millions of new people had been added to the world. And these were new people, because they would not have survived beyond age five were it not for the new health practices that kept them alive.

These new hundreds of millions needed more of the basic foods—meat and bread and cereals. But by the early 1970's, the bulging grain elevators in the United States, Canada, and Russia had been emptied. The grain crops in western Europe proved inadequate. Rice production in India and Indonesia, after rising sharply, fell short of expectation.

This shortage of the cereal and forage grasses spelled hunger, especially in the more densely populated countries of the developing nations.

Currently, popular opinion calls for a revolution in grass production. But plant specialists, economists, conservationists, and the more enlightened political figures call for a hard and practical look at the situation. "Before more grain and more forage grass and more cattle can be raised," they say, "three problems have to be recognized and solved by the world governments and their scientists."

• Problem number 1 concerns a land-use policy with an eye on increased grain production. This involves decisions pertaining to the *location* of our technological projects. Where, for example, shall the business centers, the new towns, and the road systems be located? Where shall the suburbs and the recreational areas be laid out? Where shall the dams and the reservoirs be built? What lands shall be reserved for the growing of grain?

This also involves priorities. Depending on its location, forty acres of good land may be used to produce four hundred bushels of corn—or those forty acres may be used for the construction of one mile of a federal four-lane divided highway.

Additionally, a sound land-use policy would focus on high-level utilization of the natural grasslands—the savannas and the pampas, the prairies and the steppes, as well as the open areas that are now being eyed by urban developers and strip miners.

• Problem number 2 concerns the development of grass seeds and agricultural technologies suitable for marginal lands, salt-laden soils, and depleted acreage.

• Problem number 3 concerns the genetic restructuring of cereal grasses. Needed are more varieties of improved, high-yielding hybrids with built-in resistance to drought and frost, to insects and to plant diseases. Needed are cereal plants with roots that (like the legumes) can produce their own nitrogen fertilizer and plants with cereal seeds that are rich in protein, digestible, and tasty. Taste is an important factor, because people everywhere find it difficult to accept strange and unfamiliar foods, no matter how nourishing they may be.

The FAO (the Food and Agricultural Organization of the United Nations) and a number of scientific laboratories around the world, as well as the various governments, are working on these problems. Their aim is to develop the dual role of grass—in food production for man and beast, and in soil production for the planet.

Other seed specialists, in the universities and agricultural stations and test farms, are studying ways to improve certain grasses for other purposes: for their aromatic oils; for their medicinal properties; for their fibers, in hope of developing better paper and cloth products; and as the answer to specific environmental problems along greenbelts and watersheds, highways and parks.

What the seed specialists are finding out, how the farmers and the economic planners are using these scientific findings, and what the grasses will mean in your life in the years to come is what this book is about.

CHAPTER 2

Grass Shapes the Course of History

The Gramineae family consists of some 7,500 species of grass. Of these, about a dozen different grasses stock the supermarkets with cereal products, sugar, and snacks. Breakfast specials feature puffed rice, cornflakes, rolled oats, cream of rye, and pearled barley. Loaves of bread share space with boxed doughnuts, muffin mixes, and pancake flour. These foods have one thing in common: They are all made from the seeds of cereal grass—rice and corn, oats and rye, wheat and barley.

A few aisles away, the shelves are laden with sturdy paper bags of sugar, bottles of syrup, and cans of molasses. These are all manufactured from the boiled sweet sap of the sugarcane. Tucked into the cooler are containers of oleo-margarine, made from the golden oil pressed out of corn kernels. And piled high on special counters flanking the cash register are millet seeds for sprouting, popcorn for snacking, bamboo shoots for salads, and six-packs of beer made, in part, from malted barley seeds.

These and other familiar foods, derived from the various grasses, supply most of the starch and sugar in our diets.

But other foods come *indirectly* from grass, supplying most of our animal protein.

When cattle, sheep, hogs, and poultry eat grass and the seeds of grass, their bodies convert it into protein-rich meat. The steaks and chops and roasts and drumsticks displayed in the meat case are foods once removed from grass. Certain other foods are twice removed from grass, including eggs from seed-eating birds, and milk, cheese, cream, and butter from grazing animals. ("Grazing" means "eating grass," as opposed to "browsing," which means "eating leaves and twigs.")

Hundreds and hundreds of nonedible products come from grass or the grazing animals that feed on it. Drugstores carry perfume extracted from East Indian lemon grass, as well as medicines, chemicals, and paper derived from other grasses. Specialty malls feature grass skirts and plaited straw baskets. Leather shops offer polished boots and saddles made of cowhide, and shoes and bags and belts of calf-, deer- and goatskin, and innumerable other leather items made from the hides of these and many other animals. Department stores advertise blankets, sweaters, coats, and yarn made of pure sheep's wool.

On sale, too, are fine furs—mink coats, sable stoles, and fox capes. The animals that supply these items do not eat grass. But their lives depend on the grass-eaters that they do eat.

Important as the grasses are to our way of life, the planet would have survived without them. Some animals would still be grazing in the fields, but they'd be feeding on different kinds of vegetation—on legumes and other non-grassy plants. Others would be browsing on leaves in the forest. Their varieties and numbers would be limited, however, because the legumes and the trees are geographically limited. They cannot grow under widely varying conditions and are not as adaptable or as widespread as the grasses.

Without the development of the grasses, these past seventy million years, our history would have been entirely different: Our lifestyle would still be primitive food gathering, an all-day activity, and our global population would be scattered and sparse.

Had the grasses never developed, there'd be fewer meat-eating animals. In all probability, mankind would still be living in the forests and along the waterways. Without grass seeds to eat, and without horses or oxen to plow and cultivate the fields, families would be foraging for food five or six hours a day, often more. At harvest time, they'd pick fruit and nuts off the trees and berries off the bushes. The rest of the year, they'd fish, net crustaceans, and snag seaweeds out of the coastal waters. Insect-eating birds, plus herbs and other greens, would add variety to the diet. But overeating and overweight, as well as a population explosion, would be unheard of.

Weather conditions being unpredictable, the limited food resources of the wild would frequently be destroyed by frost or hail. Without food reserves, hunger would be a constant experience, especially during the cold and rainy seasons. As for food storage, most green things cannot keep for any length of time without getting moldy, so man's winter diet would be confined pretty much to legumes, which keep for months and years. Cereal seeds, on the other hand, sometimes keep for centuries.

Without the grasses, our history would be telling a different kind of story. Ground transport, instead of being animal-powered, would have been limited to man's walking ability and to the amount of produce he could carry on his back or haul on hand-drawn wheels. War and conquest and settlement would have been restricted geographically to footpower. There'd have been no Genghis Khan, conquering North China and Persia with his hard-riding horsemen. There'd have been no China-bound camel caravans, meandering across the deserts to buy precious spices. There'd have been no Hannibal crossing the Alps with his crack troops and baggage-laden elephants, to overrun the Roman strongholds in the Po Valley. Napoleon's cavalry would not have thundered across the breadth of Europe. There'd have been no horse-mounted Spanish conquistadores, overwhelming the Aztecs in

Mexico, and the Incas in Peru. There'd have been no ox-drawn wagon trains rolling westward, settling the prairies, the high plains, and the Pacific coast.

Without the grasses, it would have been impossible to build great cities, with high rises and museums, shopping centers, factories, and industrial parks. Cities call for close-together living and efficient systems of transport for trading. But in a grassless world, close-together living and efficient transport could hardly be possible. Without the cereal grasses and the grazing cattle, people would, of necessity, have to live in small scattered settlements, surrounded by wide open spaces so they could personally forage for berries, legumes, and small, edible creatures, day after day after day. And without the transport power of oxen and horses, camels and burros and elephants, trade would be severely limited. There'd be no vast system of roads and highways, and no need for them.

It's possible that man might have leapfrogged the use of animal power and developed other forms of energy —waterwheels or solar collectors, or steam and gas engines. But it would have taken many more centuries before he could locate the necessary mines and oil wells on foot. It would have taken still more centuries before he could backpack the coal and iron and petroleum out of the ground, to centers where efficient tools could be fashioned. Only after proper tools were available could engines and trains and planes be produced. Only then could great cities have arisen.

Without grass, civilization as we know it would not have developed, because a grassless world can support only the most primitive of life-styles. Eskimos, living in a largely grassless world, have developed no great cities, no great trade depots, and no cultural centers of note. Spending so much time foraging for food, they have little left to develop high-level civilizations.

Why should the grasses be so important in man's life when there are tens of thousands of other kinds of plants growing on this earth? It's an intriguing question. The answer, however, is quite simple, once the nature of grass is understood.

All green plants have their own food factories, located in the leaves. The green chlorophyll in the leaves needs only water and nutrients from the soil, carbon dioxide from the air, and energy from the sun to manufacture food that the plant needs.

At this point, similarities between grasses and other green plants end, and the differences begin. It's these differences that enable grass plants to thrive in varied and even hostile environments, and that provide man with countless grass products.

• *If it's a grass, it has a round stem.* This stem may be hollow or pithy. Bamboo and most of the field grasses have hollow stems. Corn and sorghum, both cereal grasses, have pithy stems. And all grass stems are jointed, with solid rings circling the joints. If you've ever seen the common crabgrass, spreading along the roadside, you've seen these solid rings.

• *If it's a grass, the leaves grow out of the rings.* The scientific name for the rings is *nodes*. The leaves grow singly, one leaf out of each node, and alternately, on opposite sides of the stem. The lower part of the leaf, called the *sheath*, wraps around the stem. The upper part is called the *blade*.

Diversified in size and shape and texture, blades of grass may be soft and willowy, pleasant to walk on and pleasant to roll on. They may be stiffened with tiny amounts of silica, and bordered with sharp cutting edges, which can cut fingers and scratch bare legs. Some, like bluegrass leaves, are long and narrow. Those of panic grass are short and wide. The leaves of corn and cordgrass, which may be two feet long, taper to a point.

• *If it's a grass, it has a built-in capacity for survival.* Grass leaves may be cut again and again, or mowed or nibbled by grazing animals, but they will continue to grow. That's because grass leaves do not grow from their tips. They grow from the cells at the base of the sheath. When those cells multiply, in a process called *intercalary growth*, the leaves grow upward from the base, and so restore themselves. In most other plant families, the leaves grow from the tip. If those tips are cut or damaged, they cannot restore themselves; they simply have to wither away.

● *If it's a grass, it's a flowering plant and produces seeds.*
Grass flowers are usually small, odorless, and almost color-
less. They are wind-pollinated or self-pollinated. Although
some grasses flower every year, others flower irregularly
and spread by means of runners.

Most grasses produce great quantities of seeds, each one
tightly enclosed in a thin, dry outer covering called a
pericarp. It's the pericarp, possessed by few other plant
families, that enabled wild grass seeds to survive from ancient times. It's the pericarp that enables cultivated grain
seeds to keep for years in granaries when there are surpluses.

Sown by the wind and carried by running water, grass
seeds are world travelers. Vasey grass seeds have been
trapped in airplane scoops at a height of four thousand
feet. Seeds of grasses growing alongside riverbanks have
taken root in deltas a thousand miles downstream. Grass
seeds are carried by flying birds and wandering cattle and,

Bermuda grass was stuffed into mattresses and brought to the States in the holds of
slave ships. Now it provides bounteous hay harvests for cattle. *USDA–SCS photo.*

unknowingly, by people. Bermuda grass, stuffed into mattresses, was brought to the New World in the holds of African slave ships. Bluegrass, a native of ancient Rome, came down the Ohio River in the 1600's on cattle flatboats with the French missionaries. And some of the Turkish grasses, brought home to England by the returning Crusaders, were later brought to New England and across the United States to grow in the fields of California.

Weather and climate permitting, grass seeds sprout readily. If soil conditions are satisfactory, and light is adequate, they will grow almost anywhere in the world. If they are cultivated and cared for, they produce splendid harvests of cereal seeds for man, and forage for his cattle.

● *If it's a grass, it can grow under conditions that can support few other cultivated crops.* Grass can grow on the shores of the Arctic Ocean. It can grow in marshes, on sand dunes, and up the sides of rocky mountains. Some grasses can grow on the far-flung slopes of the Andes and the

Grass can grow on sand dunes.   *USDA–SCS photo*

Himalayas; others, in regions where the summers are too short to mature other planted crops. In steeply sloped and northerly Iceland, 98 percent of all the agricultural land is green pasture, which is used by the grazing herds.

Endowed with these unique characteristics, the Gramineae family rooted and spread. In time, vast grasslands covered one fifth of the land surface of the earth. And, as these grasslands developed, so did the food base for the increasing number of grazing animals, carnivorous animals, and lastly the omnivorous human animals.

CHAPTER 3

The Grasslands Develop as a Balanced Ecosystem

The natural grasslands are ancient in origin and span every continent except Antarctica.

In the temperate zones lie the vast fertile prairies of the Mississippi Valley and Canada, the deep-soiled pampas of Argentina, and the high velds of Africa.

In the humid tropics, the grasslands are tall-grass savannas, dotted with scrubby trees and flooded by summer rains. They are the llanos of the Orinoco River Basin, the campos of Brazil, and the low velds of southern Africa.

In the more arid regions lie the sunny, windswept, short-grass steppes of Russia, the Great Plains on the eastern slopes of the North American Rockies, and the dry plains of the Australian interior.

Primitive fossil grasses, which are 25 million years old, date these grasslands geologically. These fossil grasses are buried in the North American Great Plains, thinned to shadowy impressions on Miocene rock. They appear among the scattered bones of ancient animals that once roamed those grasslands, for grasses and grazing animals evolved together.

Almost from the beginning, most of the evolving grasses were *perennials*. Perennial grasses (like perennial rose bushes in the park) live for many years. It was the perennial grasses that transformed the ancient, raw lands into lush green grasslands. This transformation was made possible by two great groups of perennials: the *bunchgrasses*, which grow in tufts or tussocks, and the *runner grasses*, which are sod formers.

Both bunch- and runner grasses *propagate* or reproduce in two ways—by scattering seeds or by reproducing vegetatively.

When bunchgrasses reproduce vegetatively, they *tiller*—that is, they send up new stems and new shoots that enlarge the old ones, or form new ones.

When runner grasses reproduce vegetatively, they spread horizontally, by means of long stems. Some stems run underground and are called *rhizomes*. Others run aboveground and are called *stolons*. Rhizomes and stolons extend the plant's territory. They take root and send up new stems and new leaves from little buds. These grow into new plants all around the parent plant. In turn, these new grass plants send out their own runners and repeat the process.

Throughout the millennia, bunch- and runner grasses multiplied and spread. In this way, they covered millions of acres with a tough and tangled sod, and so created the grasslands.

And throughout those millennia, animals grazed there and trampled those grasslands.

Ecologically, the grazing animals and the grasslands formed a balanced interrelationship. The grasses and the wide-open spaces provided home and food for the animals. The animals, on their part, stimulated the grasses to grow thicker and more abundantly.

Because of the grazing animals, the grasslands were enriched and improved in a number of ways:

As the animals grazed, they cropped the tops off the grass leaves. This triggered the growth cells at the base of the plant, and the cropped leaves then grew long again. Cropping also caused the plants to multiply, because it

Side oats grama, a bunchgrass.   *USDA–SCS photo*

stimulated the buds at the lower nodes to produce more shoots. And these new shoots grew into new plants.

In those long-ago millennia, when there were relatively few animals, even the trampling induced grass growth. Under the animals' feet, the creeping rhizomes and stolons often broke apart, and the old runners generally rooted at the break. Then two plants, which had not been there before, developed and grew and sent out their own runners, which produced more new grass plants. And so the grass grew ever thicker under the trampling of the buffalo on the North American prairies, the antelopes on the African velds, the rheas on the Argentine; and the kangaroos in the Australian interior.

And as those animals grazed, they also fertilized the

Buffalo grass, a sod former, reproduces and spreads by way of aboveground runners called stolons.   *USDA–SCS photo*

grasslands with their dung and urine. In this way, they returned to the soil some of the phosphorus, potassium, and nitrogen that they had drawn from the grass and that the grass had drawn from the soil. When they died, their bones further enriched the soil with calcium and other minerals.

So it was that the grasslands evolved on this planet. From the thin, scraggly cover of 25 million years ago, they developed into prairies and pampas and high velds, or steppes and savannas and low velds. In varying degree, the sod grew ever thicker and denser. And the soil beneath grew more fertile. It was stirred and loosened and held in place by a fibrous network of roots. It was built up by the withered leaves of grass, the decaying, cast-off roots, the activity of great bacterial colonies, and the residue of burrowing insects and other underground animals. These

Switch grass, also a sod former, spreads by way of short underground runners or stems called rhizomes.

USDA–SCS photo

leaves and cast-off roots, these dead insects and animals were organic materials. In time, these organic materials decomposed, and in decomposing they formed a layer of rich, dark-brown humus.

When humus is worked into the soil by the activity of insects, worms, and other small creatures, the soil is enriched with organic nutrients. In addition, other qualities of the soil are improved: Sandy soils acquire more "body"; heavy clay soils become loose and porous. With enough humus in it, the soil becomes fine and fertile *topsoil*, which absorbs water well, thereby reducing the parching of the land. Without humus, soil is only a mass of ground-up rock particles (like pure sand or clay) and is quite unsuited for the growing of plants.

On the grasslands, then as now, humus formed quickly wherever the vegetation was lush. Topsoil, however, formed slowly. In some areas it took as much as a thousand years for one inch of topsoil to form.

Even as the sods and the soils of the grasslands evolved, so did the animals that grazed them. In the beginning, the animals that wandered onto the grasslands were *browsers* from the distant lands of bush and shrub. Their teeth were soft and dentine-filled, adapted to chewing the large, fleshy leaves of shrubs. At first, the tough, fibrous grass leaves, which contained (and still contain) minute quantities of hard, glassy silica, wore down these soft teeth. As the eons passed, however, the browsers shed that problem. The fossil record shows that hard teeth suitable for grazing the grasslands evolved. They were filled with cement instead of dentine, were elongated, and, like the grasses, they grew continuously from the base. If the top of a tooth broke or wore away, the tooth simply grew longer.

Those browsers evolved into successful grazers about twelve million years ago. By that time, the grasslands had become well established with grass plants and grass seeds and wildlife—similar to some that may be found in our fields, today.

Millennium after millennium, the grasslands thrived in a supportive ecosystem. It was a balanced world of plants and animals, organic remains, soil and water and minerals and air. And since the environment remained fairly stable, so did the grasslands.

Under normal conditions, grasslands continue to exist as long as the upper layer of soil gets enough rain to remain moist for a good portion of the year. If, however, the deeper layers become saturated during the annual growing seasons, and stay saturated, then deep-rooting plants like trees sometimes take over. The trees shade out the grass. The grasses weaken and die away. And as the trees continue to flourish, the area changes from grassland to woodland.

Under different conditions, a grassland might go the other way, and change to a semidesert or a wasteland. If the water table falls so low that a dry layer of soil separates it from the roots of the well-established grasses, the water-starved grass plants wither and die. Then scraggly short grasses and shrubs that require very little water invade the area. In a few years, the grassland is no more, replaced by a wasteland of shifting sands.

Another factor that supported grassland permanence was fire. Throughout the ages summer lightning storms occasionally fired the grasslands. Quick blazes, racing through the yellowed leaves of grass and the inflammable woody reeds, periodically cleared the grasslands of debris and, at the same time, killed off the young trees. The grasses, however, generally remained unharmed, because their lowermost buds, which grew close to and underneath the ground, usually escaped the racing burnover. And, many seeds, having already matured and fallen into the deep sod, also escaped burning. Later, with the first rainfall, the buds sent up new shoots, the seeds rooted, and the grasslands grew green again. Only when the fires were particularly intense and prolonged and the soil was badly burned was the greening delayed for a season or two.

Then man appeared on the scene.

Man looked at the grassland—at the thickly tufted bunchgrasses and the dense sod-forming runner grasses, all punctuated with the wild and scattered annuals, the cereal grasses.

Man liked what he saw. He saw lush pastures for herds of cattle. He saw broad valleys and black-soiled plains for crops of cereal grass. He saw bread and meat on his table.

Because man liked what he saw, the grasslands were forever after to be changed. Some were to be destroyed. Some were to be misused. Some were to be improved—remarkably. And some new grasslands, yet to be created, were to carry the man-made stamp.

Forever after, the ecosystem of grass and grazing animals was to be changed, never to be the same again.

And man's diet was never to be quite the same, either. It was to be based increasingly on greater and greater plantings of cereal grasses, which by design were to replace the wild grasses of the natural grasslands.

CHAPTER 4

The Grasses:
Food and Drink for People

By the middle of the twentieth century, the world's grasslands were producing according to design:

In the United States, Canada, Argentina, Australia, and the Soviet Union, cowboys were riding herd on the semi-arid ranges.

On the prairies and plains and river valleys, clattering combines, their drivers gritty with chaff and dust, were harvesting wheat for bread, corn for hogs, and oats for horses.

In the subtropical belt, peasants, ankle deep in mud, were draining the paddies, cutting the rice plants, hand-threshing the grain, and lugging the heavy baskets to market.

And on each of these grasslands other men—small operators with their private pot stills and scientific experts with giant industrial plants—were producing alcohol. Invariably, distillers used the native grains, those that were plentiful and cheap in the area. Some they malted for beer. Some they fermented and distilled for hard liquor.

Beer is brewed almost everywhere, but it was the United

States, with its prodigious harvests, that supplied the corn for most of the world's bourbon, and the wheat for whiskey.

At this point economists, conservationists, and the more informed political leaders began to be nagged by a statement, made three quarters of a century ago, on the floor of the United States Senate. John James Ingalls, senator from Kansas, was speaking on his favorite topic, grass, and he startled his audience with these words: "Should its harvest fail for a single year, famine would depopulate the world."
It is still a startling statement, but is it true or false?
The statement is true. For its very survival, the enormous human family is very much dependent on an *uninterrupted* harvest. But should the harvest fail . . .
In the developing countries today, nine out of every ten people already know at first hand what a failed harvest means, because they live almost entirely on grain. Bits of chicken or fish or nuts or vegetables add flavor and nourishment to the grain bowl. Even so, they receive only 75 percent of the calories they need and 40 to 70 percent of the protein. It's an inadequate diet but the only one they can afford. And they would not even have that much food if it weren't for the native cereal grasses that, though not overly abundant, thrive in their part of the world—when the harvests don't fail.
Of the great grain staples currently cultivated, it's wheat and rice and corn, the Big Three, that feed most of the world's people. Then come the secondary grains: sorghums and millets, oats and barley and rye. And, of course, there's that sweet grass sugarcane, which is a global favorite.
Under natural conditions, each of these grasses has its own particular environment, its own particular habitat, its own geographic address on Planet Earth. Each species grows best where the geography is favorable to its particular needs, in the matter of temperature and moisture, soil conditions, and hours of sunlight.

CHAPTER 5

The Food Grasses: Wheat and Corn

Wheat and *corn*, two of the major cereal grasses, grow in temperate climates.

So extensively do wheat fields girdle the planet that the sun never sets on them. It may shine on a planting of seeds in the United States, Canada, China, and the Soviet Union on the same day that it shines on farmhands and pretty girls celebrating a harvest festival in Argentina and Australia.

More people are nourished by wheat than by any other cereal grain. There are two good reasons for that: It grows abundantly, and it makes the best bread.

Wherever you find homemakers and commercial bread bakers who are proud of their light and crusty loaves, you can be sure they use wheat flour because it contains more *gluten* than any other flour. It's gluten (a protein substance) that makes bread dough smooth and elastic. When the dough is well leavened, the yeast releases harmless bubbles of carbon dioxide gas. These bubbles are trapped inside the doughy mass. They push against the dough. The dough rises. And the risen dough, placed in a preheated oven, bakes into a fine loaf that's full of little bubble holes.

Of course, good and nutritious breads can be made from other flours: from corn and rye, oats and barley, even from sorghum and millet. But those breads, though richly flavored, are often dark and heavy and closely textured, requiring strong teeth for chewing. When bakers mix those flours with wheat, half and half, some fine gourmet breads come sliding out of the oven—tasty and not too heavy. Most people, however, seem to prefer bread made from wheat flour.

There are many kinds of wheat bread. Some are pure white. Some are light brown. Some are dark brown. The color of the bread depends on the color of the flour, and that depends on the part of the seed it comes from.

The wheat kernel, which contains starch, fat, and protein, plus vitamins and minerals, is made up of three parts. The hard, brown outer covering is the *bran*. The white part, called the *endosperm*, is the starchy inside. The *embryo*, which is also called the *wheat germ*, is the part which, if planted, grows into roots, stem, and leaves.

The wheat kernel

cross section of a wheat kernel

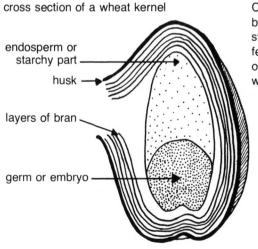

endosperm or starchy part

husk

layers of bran

germ or embryo

Components of a standard bushel of wheat:

starch	55%	30.8 lbs.
feed	26%	14.5 lbs.
oil	3%	1.7 lbs.
water	16%	9 lbs.

When the miller grinds a sack of wheat kernels, he gets whole-wheat flour. This flour, accordingly, contains all the nutrients. When he wants white flour, he grinds the whole-wheat flour a number of times. When it is very fine, he sifts it and air-blows it till all the dark bran and wheat germ have been separated out, and only the white flour (which is virtually all starch) is left. The bran and the wheat germ he sells separately—in most instances to farmers who are particular about the health of their animals.

Brown or white, bread is baked in distinctive shapes in different countries. French bakers turn out thin, white crusty breads, a yard long. Portuguese homemakers favor the large, twisted rings. Jewish ones make braided hallah for the Sabbath. And the dark round loaf is still the hallmark of a well-prepared Hungarian meal.

In the main, the wheats thrive best in the dark, rich soil of the temperate regions. They grow between the thirtieth and fifty-fifth parallels—30 and 55 degrees north latitude—in the Northern Hemisphere, and between the thirtieth and fortieth parallels—30 and 40 degrees south latitude—in the Southern Hemisphere. These are the breadbaskets of the world, where modern civilization has developed.

No one knows exactly when wheat first became important to man. Einkorn wheat, a weedy plant with small seeds and tight husks, first appeared in the Near East about ten thousand years ago. By 7000 B.C., there were thick stands of einkorn greening the basaltic cobble of Turkey, Iran, and Iraq. Shortly afterward, according to archaeologists, Late Stone Age people were gathering these seeds.

At about this time, a fortuitous natural event occurred. Some of the einkorns *crossed* with a wild goat grass and the result was emmer wheat, which was a fertile *hybrid*. (See Chapter 12 for an explanation of crossing and hybridization.) The plump emmer seeds fell easily from the seed head and rode the wind. They flew and fell and rooted and spread, till great crops of emmer were growing throughout the Middle East, and families began to settle in temporary villages around the ancient spring at Jericho and the shores of Lake Galilee.

Then another great natural event occurred. Some of the emmers crossed with another common goat grass and produced a still finer hybrid. This was *bread wheat* with its high gluten content. And with the bread wheat the story of agriculture begins.

Now the human family could gather the seeds of bread wheat, pound them into flour, and make bread. But bread wheats were scarce, because the plants did not spread from field to field. Their seed heads formed up tightly, and when they did break apart, the chaff blew away, but the heavy seeds fell in place and took root there. If man wanted more of those good bread wheats, he had to become a farmer and plant them.

And so a partnership was formed. Man cultivated the plants and harvested the seeds. The seeds provided flour for bread, and the bread provided energy. It was that energy which enabled those early civilizations to develop.

In time, this partnership grew into big business. By 2500 B.C., robed and bearded Mesopotamians were inscribing clay tablets with records of shipments to such faraway places now known as England and France. Centuries later in Rome, slaves, whitened by clouds of flour dust, were turning huge millstones and grinding wheat into flour for the public bakeries. By the time of Caesar, the sound of grinding millstones was heard along the shores of the Mediterranean, where wheat was being cultivated extensively. And after Columbus discovered America, those millions of immigrants who left the Old World for the New carried with them little sacks of wheat seeds to make sure they'd have good bread in their new homes.

Today, the United States is second only to the Soviet Union in wheat production. A hundred years ago, however, the picture was altogether different. There were no native wheats growing on the prairies, and those "immigrant" wheats planted by the settlers could not adapt to the new growing conditions—to the fiercely hot summers, to the blasting cold winters, and to the local plant diseases. Year after year, there was desolation on many fields as rust (a fungus disease) withered the crops, drought desiccated them, and early frosts blackened them.

Mark Carlton, working for the U.S. Department of Agriculture, was to change all that. In the middle of the 1890's, while inspecting the nation's crops, which were being destroyed that summer by rust and hot weather, Carlton came across a magnificent eighty-acre stand of wheat in Kansas. This wheat belonged to a group of Mennonites who had brought their seeds with them from Russia. After that, nothing would do but that Carlton must go to Russia, to the dry-as-dust Turgay Steppes. There he found the *kubanka,* a bearded hard durum wheat, being cultivated by the Khirgiz, in heat that matched that of Death Valley in July.

This kubanka, planted in the United States the next spring, soon transformed the western semiarid edge of the prairies, from North Dakota to Texas. Kubanka was drought resistant. It was high yielding. And it ripened early, days before the first frosts of autumn.

Two years later, Carlton was back in Russia, looking for winter wheat. He wanted to find a variety that could withstand the bitter winters of Kansas, Nebraska, Oklahoma, and Montana. In droshkys and on foot he explored the northern fields around Leningrad, then known as St. Petersburg. He wandered over the windswept steppes north of Odessa. He asked a thousand times in his broken Russian, "Where? Where are the winter wheats that can survive the coldest weather?"

In Starobel'sk, he found the *kharkov,* a hard red winter wheat that sinks its roots deep in the soil in autumn and is unaffected by winter, no matter how low the temperature drops.

The kharkov wheat thrived in the United States, so that by 1914 and all through the First World War, American grain ships were carrying unlimited supplies of kubanka and kharkov wheats to the Allies.

It's the kharkov, plus a number of newly developed winter wheats capable of thriving over a wider territory, that now put bread and meat on the American table. The meat comes from the cattle that are turned out, in the fall of the year, to graze on the newly sprouted wheat. Several months later, the cattle, plump and well-fed, are sent along to the feedlots for further fattening, then to the slaughter pens, and finally to the meat-processing plants.

In the meantime, the hard red winter wheats keep growing. When spring comes, dusting by plane protects them from insects and disease. In Texas, the crop is ready to harvest in mid-May. In Oklahoma, harvesting begins in June. The line of harvest moves ever northward. By September, the harvesting crews reach the Canadian border. So extensive are these American wheat fields that for many thousands of families and hired hands harvesting has become a way of life.

In May, when the wind hisses through the ripening winter wheat, some two thousand professional harvesting crews rendezvous in north-central Texas. They come with house trailers and trucks and, on top of the trucks, their combines, which will reap and thresh the grain in one operation. If it's a good year and they're facing a bumper crop, the crews (made up of field hands and college boys) know they will have to work those combines long hours —often by moonlight, more often by the blaze of their headlights. During the harvesting season, there will be no letup, no time out, and no days off. When the wheat is ready to be cut, it has to be cut. Who knows when rain or hail will flatten the grain? Who knows when a spark from an exhaust pipe or a cigarette will start a wild wheat fire? And if those disasters do not strike, a few days' delay may still mean that the crop dries out and is spoiled.

Work begins at sunrise. The combine operator hops into his air-conditioned cab, knowing he mustn't let his attention wander, not even for a minute. He must adjust the cutting bar just so; otherwise he'll either miss the seed heads or scrape the ground, pick up a stone, and jam his machine. And he must maintain proper speed. If he runs too slow, he'll be called on his two-way radio because he's losing the race against the weather. If he runs too fast, bunches of cut stalks will slip through, unthreshed.

The combine moves, and the cutting bar mows a twenty-foot swath around the field. The paddle reel churns the cut wheat onto the platform. The wheat moves into the metal maw. The seeds are knocked off and poured into the trailing truck, to be carted to the grain elevators. At the same time, the chaff is blown out to the fields, in an endless fog of dust.

A combine harvesting wheat in Nebraska.   *USDA–SCS photo*

On a good day, a single combine may shave as much as a hundred acres of standing wheat. It threshes the grain at the rate of a bushel every twenty seconds. It moves northward about a mile an hour, 15 miles a day, 450 miles a month.

In the trade, wheats are classified as hard or soft, as red or white. White wheats are favored for pastries and breakfast cereals. Durum, a hard red wheat rich in protein, is preferred for spaghetti and macaroni. Hard red wheat, straight or blended with soft, is used by bread bakers. And the balance of the soft wheat is generally diverted to farmers in hundred-pound burlap bags to be used as animal feed.

Wheat is big business where modern agricultural technology is used. But in north India and Ethiopia, in the mountains of Chile and Afghanistan, and other less-developed countries, there are farmers who continue to till their fields in the old traditional ways. They still sow the seeds broadcast—that is, they cast them out onto the ground in a broad, sweeping motion—from a bag slung over the shoulder. They still cut the ripened plants with a curved sickle, and remove them from the field with an ox-drawn sledge. They still thresh the grain with sticks or swinging flails and winnow it by hand. Even so, increased productivity is achieved when, with the guidance of the FAO (the Food and Agricultural Organization of the United Nations), the farmers use selected wheat seeds and fertilizer.

Wheat is not only big business. It is the world's number-one cereal—first in the number of acres planted, in the number of bushels produced, and in the number of pounds consumed every year.

The world's number-two grain is rice, but rice does not grow in temperate climes. It's the number-three grain, corn, that is wheat's partner. Corn thrives best in soil that is deep and dark and stoneless, hot sun, and abundant rainfall.

Everybody likes corn. And just as wheat is often eaten out of the hand—as bread—so, too, is corn, but in another way. Among Latin Americans, tortillas, enchiladas, and tacos are all eaten out of the hand, as their kind of bread. All three are made the same way, to the sound of slapping palms. The cook stirs up a batch of cornmeal, pinches off a

In Afghanistan—bringing in the harvest on an ox-drawn sledge.   *WFP/FAO photo*

In Afghanistan—winnowing in the traditional way. *AID photo*

small piece of dough, and slaps-slaps it between her palms till it looks like a thin, round pancake. This she bakes flat over a charcoal brazier. Then, if it's bent to scoop up food from the plate, it's a tortilla. If it's rolled and filled with bits of meat and sauce, it's an enchilada. If it's folded into the shape of a turnover, fried and filled, it's a taco.

Corn is good to eat—on the cob, as chowder, as popcorn, and in a dozen different ways. In the affluent Western world, however, only a very small percentage of the corn

Andean Indian farmer achieves good results using selected wheat seeds and fertilizer.
FAO photo

crop is eaten by people. Most of it is fed to hogs and poultry, in sharp contrast to the less-developed countries, where corn is the staple of food for the people. Should the harvests fail in those countries, the more prosperous nations are called on to donate or sell what's needed. And in short order, mountains of bulging brown bags, stamped "Corn . . . USA" or "Argentina," or "Canada," or "FAO, the United Nations" are piled up on the docks of the needy countries where the children stand by, rattling their empty bowls.

Corn is a New World native, completely unknown to the ancient Europeans, Asians, and Africans. Not even Marco

Polo, that famous traveler, ever came across an ear of corn. But Columbus did, on his first voyage to the West Indies. His men acquired a basket of grain from a native Indian who called it *ma-hiz*. (And maize it was to become to the people of Europe and, in fact, to the later botanists, who classified it as *Zea mays*.) Columbus named the gift seeds Indian grain or—the word "corn" meaning the same then as "grain"—Indian corn.

The next year, when he returned from the islands, Columbus carried baskets of corn back to Spain in the ship's hold. Within a few years, corn was being cultivated in kitchen gardens throughout Europe. In the early 1500's, Spanish and Portuguese sailors traded, bartered, and sold corn seeds to the natives in Africa and India. By 1540, even the Chinese, having hauled baskets of seed corn over the mountains of Tibet, were cultivating their own cornfields. Soon corn was a familiar crop almost everywhere around the world.

Of course, corn had long been cultivated by Indians throughout the Americas. Magellan found it growing in the region of Rio de Janeiro. De Soto saw it growing along the Mississippi. Champlain discovered it in New England. Miles Standish found it when searching for food for the Pilgrims.

From coast to coast, from the Atlantic to the Pacific, the American colonists, heading west, could count on roasted ears of corn around the campfire. Farmers all along the trail were raising corn in neat, well-plowed fields. Trappers in the woodlands were raising corn in small clearings. Along the shores of the Great Lakes fishermen planted corn for the winter. And wherever they came upon an Indian village, of course, they found cornfields surrounding it, perhaps guarded by dark-faced little Indian girls, who clutched corn-husk dolls as they chased away marauding birds.

The varieties of corn were legion. Some produced ears no more than two inches in length. Others produced ears almost two feet long. There were ears with white kernels and black, with red and yellow and blue. And some were altogether multi-colored.

There was *dent* corn, so called because of the little dent in each kernel, caused by the unequal drying of the hard and soft starches. *Sweet* corn contained more sugar than starch. *Flint* corn had very hard kernels. Two other kinds were especially preferred by the Indians: *flour* corn, which was sometimes parched and taken along on hunting trips, and sometimes ground into soft flour, and *popcorn*. A scooped-out pit in the ground, a fire in the pit, and sand tossed on the fire summoned the tribe to a popcorn feast. Then the hot sand was shoveled into a pottery jar, covered with a handful of popcorn kernels, and capped. As the kernels got hotter, the moisture in each one built up to steam until it exploded. When the crackling quieted, the corn was ready to eat.

Strange as it may seem, the corn plant is dependent on man for its very survival. It's unlikely that a modern corn plant would be able to reseed itself. The husks are so tight, and the kernels so firmly embedded in the cobs, that it would take years for them to loosen and fall out naturally. Then, if the rodents and the bacteria and the mold hadn't already destroyed them, all the clumped-together kernels would begin to sprout where they fell. And in a short time they'd all crowd each other out of the picture.

If corn is to grow to maturity, the seeds have to be planted and cared for. In Mexico, Guatemala, Chile, and the less-developed countries of Asia and Africa, these plantings are, for the most part, still done the old way, on farms ranging from half an acre to five acres. In the spring, the families haul the sacks of seed corn from their storage cribs out to the fields. They plant them, three or four seeds to a hill. Later, they hoe the soil around the young stalks to keep the weeds down. Still later, they pull the ripened ears by hand. This is slow, hard work and produces limited harvests.

By contrast, corn grows almost automatically for the farmers in the technologically advanced countries, who in the main specialize in hybrid corn. In the spring, one man, riding his tractor across the fields, plants twelve rows at a time, simultaneously spraying them with the necessary chemicals—fertilizers, herbicides, and fungicides. In the

In an American cornfield a big ear is the usual thing.   *USDA–SCS photo*

fall, in a flurry of activity, mechanical corn pickers strip the ears from the stalks, shell the kernels, and pour them into trucks, to be carted away to a corn dryer, after which, they go to the storage depots or the mills. In the fall, too, the specialized seed companies begin their annual harvesting of hybrid seed corn. (See Chapter 12.)

In the Western world, the size of the cornfields is limited only by the available acreage of suitable land, because the world market is wide open. An aerial photographer, flying over the north-central American states, can photomap cornfields for hundreds upon hundreds of miles. In each field, the plants are the same size because they are hybrids with a built-in timetable for growth. In spring, the flying photographer snaps the fields, sprouting green. In summer, his camera shows the plants tall and tasseled. In the fall he catches them turning brown, dry and papery. And whenever his plane flies low over Chicago, there, topped by a statue of Ceres, the Roman Goddess of Grain, is the Board of Trade Building, which houses the biggest, the noisiest grain market in the world. It's a market that's full of shouting brokers, clicking computers, and the Big

Board, flashing the changing prices per bushel of corn.

In the United States, that part of the corn crop which is not fed to livestock is processed for food and industrial purposes. In the southern "dry mills," white dent kernels are ground into coarse meal for making spoon bread, a soft puddinglike dish. In the northern refineries, they change the milling process somewhat and produce hominy grits, cornmeal, and flour. Brewers buy up most of the grits for malting. Housewives buy the cornmeal for baking Indian pudding in New England, and for boiling scrapple in Pennsylvania. The flour finds its way into breakfast foods, pancake mixes, and confections.

In other refineries, "wet millers" steep the shelled corn in warm water vats to facilitate the processing for oil, starch, gluten, and bran.

Starch is the main component of the corn kernel. Some of it is converted into syrup and corn sugar. The demand for corn syrup is so great that it is delivered in tank trucks to such establishments as commercial bakeries, tobacco-curing plants, and rayon factories, where it is pumped into storage tanks. And the sugar, in the form of dextrose, is used among other things for intravenous feedings.

In the industrial world, starch processed from corn is used in the making of thousands of things—from lollypops to airplane parts, from paper and laminated playing cards to dynamite and baking powder, twine, batteries, and shotgun shells. In the home, starch is used to thicken pies, puddings, and sauce. In the laundry, it stiffens cottons.

A small part of the corn crop is also fermented as industrial alcohol and used to drive motor cars. And another part is fermented as a sour mash, distilled, and bottled as bourbon.

For many in the Western world, there's magic in a cornfield, but for many of the world's perpetual poor, corn continues to be the chief staple of food.

CHAPTER 6

The Food Grasses: Oats, Barley, and Rye

Three other great cereal grasses thrive abundantly in the temperate zones, but prefer a cooler climate than wheat and corn. These are oats, which rank as the number-four grain, and barley and rye.

Oats are very nutritious, being higher in special protein than any other cereal. Yet oats are more often found in a horse's feedbag than in a child's cereal bowl.

The United States and Canada raise tremendous quantities of this cereal grass, 50 percent of the global harvest. Yet only 5 percent of it is eaten by people. Low in gluten, oats alone do not make good bread, but they can be enjoyed as oatmeal porridge or oatmeal cookies. Across the sea, the Scots, who are devoted to oats, make innumerable puddings, drinks, and cakes of this grain, including the awesome concoction known as haggis. The English prefer to feed oats to their horses and use the straw for bedding them down.

When conditions are right, it's no problem for a farmer to raise a bumper crop of oats. Given fifteen inches of rain per year and a cool climate (such as is found in Canada and the northern regions of the United States, Europe, and Asia) the fields yield great quantities of white or common oats. This is the kind that's processed as quick-cooking, rolled, or steel-cut oats. Red oats, however, the kind that is fed to horses and cattle, grow better in the warmer areas, in the American Gulf States, along the Mediterranean shores, and in Australia. Additionally, oats may be planted as green pasture for the grazing animals. They may also be planted as a "companion crop" together with alfalfa. Oats are quick growing. Alfalfa is not. The oat plants, accordingly, grow rapidly and shade the slow-growing tender alfalfa shoots. Later, after the oat crop has been harvested, the alfalfa continues to grow, and by the following summer provides a splendid crop of its own.

If oats are so nutritious and so easily grown, one wonders why it isn't more of a popular favorite. The answer lies in tradition.

Traditionally, oats were considered to be weeds that invaded the barley fields. As such a nuisance, they were considered unfit for human consumption. It wasn't until the Bronze Age that Germanic tribes began to separate the oats from the barley and plant them on a large scale. In the fall, after they cut the oat plants, they flailed them to knock off the seeds, then winnowed the seeds to separate them from the chaff. After that, they crushed the seeds and cooked them as porridge. At about the same time, the Romans to the south began growing oats for their horses. Later, when the Germans overran the city of Rome, they were cynically called "those oat-eating barbarians."

Eating habits change slowly. Few people who had not been raised on oatmeal would think of ordering it in a restaurant. Still, slowly but surely, more oats are being incorporated into the human diet. Some oats are ground into flour and used to keep certain foods from turning rancid. Added to candy mixes, pie crusts, potato chips, and butter, oat flour keeps them from spoiling. And dusted inside cookie tins, it keeps them fresh longer.

Actually, the entire oat crop adds considerably, though indirectly, to the human food base. Although the greater part of it is fed to cattle and poultry, isn't that where our

meat and milk and cream and poultry products come from?
The next time you enjoy a bowl of chicken soup, you can
be pretty sure that the chicken had enjoyed more than a
handful of oats. The next time, too, that you see a bottle of
whiskey, in some specialty food and drink shop, you
can be pretty sure it was distilled from an old Celtic recipe
dating back to 1100—distilled from oats and barley malt.

Barley can tolerate a multiplicity of environments. Although the various types are now cultivated in different
countries, the primitive wild barley still grows in its original
habitat.

In the fields of southeast Turkey, a little girl can still fill
her apron with wild barley seeds for her mother to grind
up for barley bread. On the slopes of the Zagros Mountains, an Iraqui boy can still grab a fistful of wild barley
plants and race them home to his penned-up chickens.
And for their daily porridge, the very poor in Iran continue
to gather barley grains that grow along the roadsides and
on the rooftops of their mud huts.

Even now, wild barley grows in massive stands in parts
of the Middle East—in Israel and Jordan, in Syria and
around Baku in the Soviet Union. And in the wadis, along
the desert's edge, there are still Bedouin tribes who cultivate limited harvests of wild barley. These are the two-
rowed plants, with two rows of kernels on each seed head.
The cultivated variety contains six rows and consequently
is a heavier yielder.

Cultivated barley grows like cultivated wheat and, like
wheat, may be planted in the fall or in the spring. Unlike
wheat, barley isn't fussy about temperature or rainfall or
soil. It can grow in the poorest of alkaline soils, where no
other cereal grasses could grow. Barley is also so frost resistant that it thrives beyond the Arctic Circle and along the
shores of frozen ponds. It grows on the Himalayan slopes
at fifteen thousand feet above sea level. And, being also
drought resistant, it grows well on the dry plains of India,
in arid Australia, and in the desert, under the palm trees.

Wherever it grows, most of the barley harvest is bagged
for the farms, for the livestock feed bins. The rest is re-

served for human consumption, some of it for food, some for drink.

If you've ever dined on barley soup or a steaming dish of buttered pearl barley, you know what these seeds taste like. If you've ever enjoyed a malted milkshake, you've enjoyed barley in the form of malt extract.

To malt barley, the maltster heaps the seeds in an enormous vessel and soaks them till they soften. Then he dumps them on the floor of the malting house. Periodically, he sprinkles them with warm water till they begin to germinate. The germinating seeds, which are called malt, undergo a chemical change, which turns their starch to sugar. In about three weeks, after the malt is entangled in a mass of sprouts and rootlets, it is dried in a kiln, then screened. The sprouts and rootlets are removed. The malted barley seeds are crushed. And the resulting liquid, called malt extract, is used in the making of malted milkshakes, beer, some breakfast cereals, and Scotch whiskey.

It takes a number of steps to turn raw barley into Scotch. In the first step, the brewmaster malts the barley. In the second, he mashes it—meaning that he grinds the malt and mixes it with warm water in a mashing tub. When it begins to smell distinctively (like nothing else on earth), the brewmaster draws it off to the still (short for "distillery") and mixes it with a bit of yeast to encourage fermentation. In due time, the fermented mixture is distilled—not once, but several times. After that it is diluted with good quality water to a proof of 124 or 126, and finally, it is run into white-oak casks and left to mature.

That's barley, a cereal grain which has been used as food and drink since ancient days. As a food, it is mentioned in the Bible many times, because people in those days lived largely on barley bread. It was a dense and heavy bread, because barley seeds contain little gluten. It's the same kind of bread that the little Turkish girl, mentioned at the beginning of this chapter, might be eating today. And, as a drink, barley is mentioned in Old English literature dating back to the 1500's. It was probably the first cereal grain to be malted and distilled on a large scale in the British Isles and western Europe.

It's very doubtful that Sweden, Norway, Finland, north-ern Russia, and Siberia would have advanced culturally to any great extent—or even been widely populated—were it not for *Secale cereale*, which is the scientific name for *rye*. It's true that oats and barley grow well in cool areas, but for the very cold and rugged northlands, the answer is rye —with its tough roots that reach down six feet.

Some varieties of rye grow at temperatures that kill off the other cereal grasses. Winter rye, planted in the fall, sprouts when the thermometer stands at a low 33 degrees Fahrenheit—one degree above freezing. And it matures when the thermometer hovers around 55. Farther north, however, winter rye may sometimes be destroyed by the bitter frosts. In those regions (as well as in some parts of Argentina), farmers prefer not to take chances with the harvest and, accordingly, concentrate on spring rye.

Some two thousand years ago, when wanderers from the Middle East and central Europe began moving northward, they found those wild rye plants growing in the fields. These they tamed—that is, they selected the best seeds every autumn and saved them for the next year's planting. The cultivated rye soon shaped the dietary customs of the northland. To this day, country meals start with dark slices of bread, thickly covered with good butter. The butter comes from the cows that graze the rye, growing in the fields and pastures. In winter, they are sustained, in part, by rye seeds and hay which the farmer stores for them.

The bread is tasty, but because it's heavy and rather dense, housewives have learned to bake assorted breads "northland style." In Sweden, they feature rye *knäckebröd*, which is baked in round disks with a hole in the middle and strung on a long pole under the ceiling. They also mix up a batch of rye flour and sour milk, roll out the dough into thin leaves, and bake it. These waferlike bread leaves are then stored in a special kind of breadbox that looks like a little chest of drawers.

In southern Norway, where oats and barley grow as readily as rye, homemakers bake multigrain crackers called *flatbrod*.

Even in Western countries, where fancy baked goods are

preferred, bread made from equal parts of rye and gluten-rich wheat flour is a great favorite.

Of the global rye crop, as much as one third is used for bread, for hardtack, rye crisps, and rye rounds for party snacks. The remainder of the crop is used for feeding livestock, for reseeding damaged lands, and for making intoxicating beverages.

Rye whiskey is distilled from a fermented rye mash. Dutch gin is made from three grains, barley malt, corn, and rye, cooked and fermented into mash, then distilled and flavored with juniper berries. Russian kvass is a kind of beer, made from rye bread with barley and malt added.

CHAPTER 7

The Food Grasses: Millet and Sorghum

People have a way of making almost any climate work for them. Where the weather is good, the land fertile, and rainfall abundant, the cereal grasses grow well, and living is simple. Where the climate is harsh, the sun scorching, the rain almost nonexistent, and the soil impoverished, man must find the cereal grasses that grow in his homeland. Two grasses that thrive in inhospitable climes are the millets and the sorghums.

One third of the global population, hundreds of millions of the world's poorest people, manage to live almost entirely off the grain that grows on those infertile lands—on the semiarid plains of India and Pakistan, north China, Manchuria, Japan, and parts of the Soviet Union, as well as certain regions in the central and western parts of Africa.

Millet has been called the poor man's cereal, because it grows where little else will grow. Millet is an ancient grass. It was, in fact, considered a holy grass in China, and was planted there by royal edict as early as 2700 B.C. The millets consist of six or seven different kinds of grass, all producing very small seeds.

56

All the millets provide good food. From the variety of millet seeds and green millet seed heads are made porridge and bread and thick cakes for eating with stew. Green millet ears are eaten like asparagus, and other forms of the grain make puddings, sticky sweets, and a kind of beer.

Actually, not all the millet varieties can be grown in the same region. But the seeds are versatile. When they're crushed and ground into meal, they can be cooked and baked. When they're malted, they make excellent beer. And they can be fed to goats and poultry, to be processed by those animals into meat and milk and eggs.

The seeds of *proso* millet were eaten by the ancient Romans, and they're still eaten in certain parts of Europe and Asia. Proso is a tall plant that thrives farther north than any other variety of millet. For centuries, it was the food staple in the dry areas of Russia, where it was cooked up as a thick porridge called Russian kasha. And because it is also a treat for the chickens, a common riddle in that part of the world goes like this: "What does a hen dream of?" The answer: "Proso, of course."

Another outstanding millet is the *pearl*. Pearl is so drought resistant, it thrives on the very edge of the desert. It's taller even than proso, as much as ten feet sometimes, though usually no more than five or six. In very hot weather, its long, flat leaves curl up to conserve moisture and retard evaporation. The distinctive thing about pearl is that it looks like the common cattail that grows in the American swamps. Its seeds are clustered thickly on stiff upright heads that extend about eighteen inches. As porridge, pearl millet is a popular dish in India. In the African Sudan, however, they like it best when it's baked into thick cakes and served with the stew, or malted as beer.

The Chinese favor the *foxtail* variety, which feeds about one fifth of their population. Additionally, foxtail seeds, when fermented with rice, produce a mildly intoxicating toddy. When the toddy is distilled, as it often is, it turns into a hard drink called *sautchoo*.

Most of the millets grow on the hot, dusty plains, but *finger* millet grows in the mountains, in the moister parts of India. Weather permitting, the Indians plant finger millet as a second crop, in the drained rice paddies, after the rice has been harvested. The seeds of this variety form on five seed heads, which grow out of the millet stem like five fingers. Often these seed heads are cut green and served as fresh vegetables. If they are allowed to ripen, their seeds, like all millet seeds, may be ground into flour for porridge or bread.

The millets have sustained many of the poor in the Middle East, the Far East, and Africa since ancient times, and they sustain many of the poor in the Third World today. But not all the poor are fed, not even when yields are abundant. Consequently, every single grain of millet is precious. Little children, very old men, and imaginative scarecrows are stationed in the millet fields to scare away the seed-eating birds. In Ethiopia, in India and China, when the seed heads begin to ripen, the children and their grandparents take their places in the fields, and yell and whistle and make threatening noises. Nevertheless, the birds manage to steal a large part of the crop.

The situation is quite different in the Western world, where much millet is raised especially for the birds. Along both sides of the Atlantic seaboard, homeowners plant tidy little plots of proso and foxtail to attract goldfinches and cardinals to their gardens. In some states, a major farm crop is millet for birds, both pet and wild. North Dakota, for example, ships a carload a day just to New York City, for its parakeets and canaries.

It was only during the past century that some of the millets were transported to the West. In the United States, they serve as an ideal crop for the Great Plains because of their resistance to drought. Additionally, pearl millet and foxtail are sown in many farm pastures as forage for the livestock. Proso, however, must be harvested early, because it is easily damaged by frost. Most farmers think of proso as hog millet, because the hogs eat it as readily as the more expensive corn.

Increasingly, American farmers are planting more acreage to the millets, for pasturage as well as for seeds for animal feed. In the Southwest, much attention is currently being given to a new pearl hybrid that yields 50 percent

An agronomist compares the longer cobs of dwarf millets grown from imported seeds with the cobs of the local variety.　　*FAO photo*

more grain than the original pearl in its native India.

The millets are far cheaper than wheat or rice or the other common cereal grains, but most Westerners would rather feed the millet seeds to their animals than eat it themselves. That's because taste is a matter of habit, and few Westerners have, as yet, acquired a taste for the flavor or the sticky texture of cooked millet. Persons interested in health foods, however, have found that *sprouted* millet seeds are delicious and nutritious and cost no more than a few cents per serving.

Like the millets, the sorghums consist of several kinds of grasses: The *grain* sorghums, raised primarily for their seeds; the *sweet* sorghums raised for their sweet sap, which is processed into syrup; the *grass* sorghums, raised for pasture and hay; and *broomcorn*, a stiff variety of sorghum that is used for making brushes and brooms.

A visitor, passing by a sorghum field, might easily mistake it for a cornfield. The stems are stiff and solid. The leaves grow out of heavy rings that circle the stems. And the plants, depending on the variety, grow from three to fifteen feet tall. Corn, however, could not grow where the native sorghums of Asia and Africa grow, because corn requires much more water. The native sorghums require so little water that they are ideally suited for the parched lands. Their waxy leaves are drought tolerant and, like the pearl millet, roll up to retard evaporation when the sun is especially scorching and the air too dry.

Nobody knows exactly when or where the sorghums originated. Egyptian records show them being cultivated

In the Yemen Arab Republic, an agronomist compares a cob of the local variety of sorghum with an Egyptian variety, grown experimentally on a project farm. The Egyptian variety produces five or six times as much grain.   *FAO photo*

east of the Nile in 2200 B.C. And Pliny, the Roman historian, mentions sorghum crops in England, Belgium, and Germany during the first century A.D. Some archaeologists are inclined to think the sorghums originated in Africa, others that they originated in India. Most agree that this is an ancient cereal grass whose seeds were gathered and crushed and eaten as porridge by the people of the Late Stone Age. In India, it is still eaten as porridge and sometimes baked as flat cakes. The Chinese like it for its nutlike flavor and cultivate their *kaolang* in regions too dry for rice culture.

With a little care, the sorghums produce two harvests from a single planting. Like some of the bunchgrasses, the sorghums tiller—that is, they send up new shoots after the first harvest; then when the shoots are grown, they produce a second crop.

Throughout the centuries, the sorghums spread to the warm areas in the temperate and tropical zones. More recently, great crops began to be raised in Australia, primarily for animal forage. In the United States, a variety called *chicken corn* was first introduced on the South Atlantic Coast in Colonial times, but it didn't persist and escaped as a weed. At the beginning of the nineteenth century, two varieties were introduced and cultivated on a couple of Indian reservations in Texas. One was a grain sorghum, the other a sweet sorghum. Both grew well—so well, that the American pioneers were greatly heartened. They had given up on corn, which would not grow in that hot, dry climate, and they were ready to move farther west. Now, with the sorghums producing bumper crops, they decided to stay, and their wives soon learned to make tasty sorghum pancakes drenched with sorghum syrup.

Today, there are more than fifty kinds of sorghum growing in the Great Plains of the United States and the dry steppes of Russia. In many instances, these sorghums have replaced the native American and Russian grasses because of their superior drought resistance.

Of all the sorghums presently growing in the States, some are imports and transplants from the East, and some are hybrids which have been developed since the 1950's.

One such hybrid, the *double dwarf*, has just about re-placed the tall varieties on the king-size Western ranches, because it is a heavier yielder and easier to harvest.

Milking cows and laying hens, fattening lambs, beef cat-tle, and swine like the taste of sorghum and thrive on it. Experiments have shown that the feed value of sorghum is about equal to that of corn.

Today, sorghum cultivation is not confined to the dry and infertile areas, because some of the high-yield hybrids have been bred to grow over wide ranges of temperature and to produce extraordinarily well if given a little irriga-tion water and some nitrogen fertilizer.

In the less-developed countries, however, the small farmers cannot afford to buy irrigation water any more than they can afford to buy fertilizer, so they must con-tinue to grow the old low-yield plants. Consequently, where men must depend on the millets and the sorghums as major crops, raising enough food continues to be a prob-lem.

CHAPTER 8

The Food Grasses: Rice and Sugar

In the mountains of Luzon, the Filipino and his young son climb up to a bamboo platform. They stamp their feet and trample the cut rice plants. The seed heads break apart, the grains loosen, and the rice sifts through the platform to the mat below.

In Thailand, Burma, and East Pakistan, in ponds flooded by the monsoons to a depth of twenty feet, farmers in rowboats are harvesting their floating rice. Sickles in hand, they sever the ripened seed heads and fill their baskets.

In the United States, huge combines thunder over the rice plantations, cutting, threshing, and readying the rice for shipment to the mills.

The annual rice harvest feeds half of the global population. In most instances, rice is eaten where it is raised, but—unlike wheat and corn, which in some form can be eaten out of the hand—rice is eaten out of a bowl. Each seed cooks up so firmly and holds its shape so well, it can be picked up with a pair of chopsticks.

Housewives generally prefer one of two kinds of rice: the long grain, which can be served as fluffy kernels, and the

short grain, which is pleasantly chewy but has a slight ten-
dency to stick together. Restaurants in Indonesia, Vietnam,
Burma, Laos, and India serve the long-grain variety. In
China, Japan, and along the Caribbean, they prefer the
short grain.

Rice grains, found in an archaeological dig in India, were
carbon-dated 3000 B.C. Mention of rice is made in a faded
Chinese manuscript that was written in 2800 B.C. By the
fourth century A.D., rice was growing in Greece from
seeds brought back by Alexander the Great from India. By
the sixteenth century, English merchants were importing
and milling great shiploads of rice from the island of
Madagascar, off the east coast of Africa. A century later,
one of those English ships, laden to the gunwales with
Madagascar rice, was blown off course by an Atlantic gale,
and landed in Charleston, South Carolina. And that's how
Carolina rice got its start in the United States.

Today, rice is cultivated wherever the growing conditions are right—hot sun and plenty of water. This is the
global belt between 37 degrees south latitude and 48 degrees north latitude. Rice flourishes along coastal plains
and river valleys and deltas that are flooded periodically,
especially along the Indus and Ganges Rivers in India, the
Irrawaddy in Burma, the Nile in Egypt, and the lower Mississippi in the United States. It grows in the swamplands
of Africa and New Guinea. It also grows in the rain-fed
paddies which are cut, layer upon layer, in the clay hills of
China and Indonesia. And it grows in paddies that are
irrigated with water that has to be paid for. There is also an
upland variety that grows quite well in dry soil, provided
some rain falls every day or nearly every day. Brazil and
parts of tropical Africa are great producers of this dry upland variety.

Traditionally, in the less-developed countries, rice has
been cultivated in the family paddies by hand or with the
aid of oxen. The seeds are first planted in soft mud. Later,
the young shoots are transplanted to the paddies and
flooded. Always, the growing rice plants must be kept im-
mersed in cooling water, otherwise the sun would shrivel
them right down to the roots. As the plants get taller,

Women transplanting rice in Ceylon.

the paddies must be flooded to higher levels, either by
irrigation or the seasonal rains. When, finally, the seed
heads are fully grown and the seeds are all nicely plumped,
the water is drained. After the plants are dried out, they
are cut with a knife or a sickle or a small hand-propelled
machine. Then they are bundled onto an A-frame and carried on the farmer's back to his home. There he beats his
harvest with sticks on a smooth floor, or tramples it, or lets
the children rub it by hand, to separate the seeds from the
straw. If he has an ox or a water buffalo, he lets the animal
do the trampling. In areas where the farmers can afford it,
they sometimes buy a communal threshing machine.

In the United States, parts of Europe, and Australia, rice
growing has been largely mechanized. Men, riding tractors

A Turkish farmer puddling the soil in his paddy, readying it for the rice plants.
FAO photo

with plows and levelers attached, ready the ground, then mound up the dikes with their pushing blades. Field hands turn on the irrigation pumps and flood the fields. Low-flying planes seed the prepared paddies. And later, when the green shoots are visible, those same planes return and drop fertilizer and insecticide into the water, which is kept at the proper level by the foreman. Two weeks before harvest time, the water is drained. When the fields are dry, huge power-driven combines roll in to cut and thresh the grain in a single operation.

Mechanized agriculture is, of course, fast and efficient. On an American rice plantation, a farmer can grow a ton of this grain in one day's worth of man-hours. In most of Asia, where the work is still done by hand, a farmer must labor a hundred day's worth of man-hours to grow the same amount—one ton.

No matter how the grain is threshed, there are always plenty of rice seeds that get bruised, shattered, and broken in the process. These seeds are not wasted. The Chinese use them for making a beer called *samshu*. The Japanese make *saké*.

Although saké is a beer, it is not malted. The brewmaster starts with a vat of *kojo*, which is steamed rice, and adds a special yeast culture plus a paste of fresh rice starch. He allows this mixture to ferment for about a month, then adds more kojo plus fresh rice and water. After more fermentation, it is ready to be filtered and poured into maturing casks. The Japanese do not drink this beer from foaming mugs. They make a ceremony of the occasion and sip it from one-ounce porcelain bowls.

There are thousands of different kinds of rice plants growing around the world, and they vary widely in size, in taste, in texture, and in food quality.

In the Orient, many people eat rice three times a day— and some of them have almost nothing else. Fortunately, rice is an extraordinarily healthful food. In its natural brown state, before it is polished, rice is the richest known source of vitamin B. For millennia, this brown rice, eaten with bits of fish or chicken, a few soybeans or peanuts, provided a good, nourishing diet for the people of the Far East. In recent decades, however, it has become fashionable to eat polished white rice, and housewives who can

Women in India harvesting the rice after the paddies are drained and dry.
WFP/FAO photo

afford it insist on buying it. They do not realize that by serving white rice to their families, they are, in the main, serving white starch and little else.

Everything of value in a kernel of brown rice—the vitamins, the bran, and the germ—is removed when the seed coat is removed. This happens at the polishing mill, which turns out rice that is beautifully white and shiny. The bran and the germ are retrieved, and later fed to livestock and poultry. We know that livestock and poultry thrive on these "rice polishings." When, however, they are fed white rice and little else, they can get just as sick as people do—when *they* eat white rice and little else.

In 1897, Christiaan Eijkman, a Dutch doctor who was assigned to a hospital in Java, was probably the first to sense the relationship between white rice and beriberi, a disease that causes inflammation of the nerves and the wasting away of arm and leg muscles. Dr. Eijkman had been working with his patients unsuccessfully when he happened to notice a flock of chickens on the hospital grounds. Like the patients, the chickens were staggering and falling. Like the patients, they were living on white rice—on the leftover grains from the cereal bowls. Perhaps this disease had something to do with the white rice? Dr. Eijkman didn't know, but he tried feeding the chickens with the brown rice hulls, and they recovered. Twenty years later, further research was to show that brown rice contained the B_1 vitamin thiamine, which was the *anti*-beriberi vitamin, and just as essential to human health as it was to the health of chickens.

Since that time, concerned governments began to require the enrichment of white rice with vitamins, especially B_1. In many countries of the Orient, however, beriberi is still a common complaint.

For that half of the world's population which subsists on rice, agricultural research teams have been developing new rice hybrids that produce more abundantly. They have also been working to improve the keeping qualities of brown rice, which turns rancid in storage, unless it is kept under refrigeration. At the same time, teams of nutrition experts are keeping a close eye on the vitamin content of this most excellent cereal grass.

Excellent though it may be, rice does not appeal equally to all people. Accordingly, consumption varies. It's about 400 pounds per capita in the Orient. (Cooked rice swells up to three times the volume of uncooked, and that's a lot of rice to eat, each and every day.) It's about 120 pounds per capita in Cuba, 15 pounds in Italy, but only 5 or 6 pounds in the United States.

Americans may consume no more than 5 or 6 pounds of rice each, per year, but they consume between 120 and 130 pounds of sugar. Most of this sugar comes from that tall grass, the sugarcane, and it averages out to 5 ounces a day. That's almost three quarters of a cup of sugar for every man, woman, and child. And yet nobody ever fills a bowl with sugar, sits down, and makes a meal of it. Sugar, unlike the cereals, is not a lifesaving food staple. It is used to add flavor and energy to other foods—to breakfast cereals, bread, cake, pancakes, ice cream, even to catsup and hot dogs. Sugar is consumed straight only in various forms of candy—rock candy (crystallized sugar), cotton candy (spun sugar), caramel (burnt sugar), and so on.

Sugar, which can be bought in any market now, was at one time totally unheard of. For sweetening, early man knew only of the honey tree. Not until the ninth century B.C. did the Chinese discover a sweetener that came from "a rare and precious plant" that grew in India. A thousand years later, a bundle of cuttings from this rare and precious plant was brought to Egypt by some enterprising Arabs who had been to India. And this bundle of cuttings, wrapped in palm leaves, tucked into a goatskin bag, and slung over the back of a plodding camel was to be the basis for the development of sugar empires around the world.

When those cuttings, which are called *setts*, were planted in Egypt's moist, rich soil, they rooted and produced new shoots. Within a year, these shoots grew into tall, leafy sugarcane plants with thick stems filled with sweet and juicy fibrous pulp.

By the eighth century A.D., thousands of barefoot fellahin were tending great sugar plantations in the Nile Valley. They planted the setts. They hand-hoed the fields. At harvest time, they slashed the tall cane stalks with their flashing knives, then hauled the stalks on camelback or on two-wheeled carts to the sugar mills. There they chopped and shredded the stalks and extracted the juice. As the juice boiled in huge open kettles, the air misted with sweet-smelling steam. Soon little crystals appeared, and the Egyptians were producing sugar.

Sugar production was a good business, because the Europeans clamored for sugar and were willing to pay well for it. Consequently, cane growing increased. It spread along the shores of the Mediterranean till it reached Spain and Portugal. And that's when the story of sugar began to change the course of history.

Columbus recognized the West Indies as a good sugar-growing habitat. On one of his return voyages to the islands, he brought some setts with him, and almost immediately a New World industry was born.

In the sixteenth century, sugarcane helped stimulate the Age of Discovery and Exploration. Gold might draw men to the New World like a glittering beacon, but it was sugar that built them solid fortunes. Once it was seen what wealth lay in growing cane, the search was on for new lands—new lands that were hot and moist, with a temperature of 70 degrees and sixty inches of rainfall, new lands that bordered the ocean for quick transport.

During the long rivalry over possession, Portugal was nudged off the sea-lanes, and the Spanish flag was hoisted over new sugar colonies in Cuba, Puerto Rico, Santo Domingo, the Philippines, and parts of modern United States. Only Brazil was to remain in Portuguese hands.

The sugar trade was so good, however, that Spain, in turn, was challenged by settlers, raiders, and pirates from other European countries, and soon sugarcane was being grown by planters speaking a variety of tongues. British, French, and Dutch Guiana, British Barbados and Jamaica, French Martinique, Dutch West Antilles, and other subtropical lands were soon shipping sugar wealth to the home countries.

Parallel with the development of sugarcane fields around the world was the introduction of slavery. Slaves provided cheap labor, and cheap labor was needed to plant the setts, cultivate the fields, harvest the sweet crop, and process the juice into sugar.

Sugarcane is a perennial grass that is allowed to grow for about four years before the fields are cleared and replanted. Reaching upward some twenty feet, the stalks carry stiff, coarse leaves, which lacerate the hands that try to strip them. It was slave labor that made sugar growing profitable in the old days. It is still profitable in such places as Puerto Rico and the Philippines, where the natives are willing to swing their machetes for low wages, although even there, hand labor is becoming a problem. Where wages are high, as in Hawaii, the American Gulf states, and Australia, the planters find it more profitable to mechanize their operations.

In Hawaii, for example, the plantations are vast. There, the roads cut through the fields of tall cane, and the "sugar people" (those skilled workers who operate the machines) plant, fertilize, and spray the setts with protective chemicals. Growing goes according to plan, with the aid of *hana-wai*, the Hawaiian term for "working water." At harvest time, more machines mow down the crop, after which tractor-drawn burners fire the dry leaves, charring them off the stalks, making them easier to load. Then a continuous convoy of trucks starts rolling to the sugar mills that dot the landscape. Derricks lift the stalks from the cagelike truck-beds and swing them inside. Thundering machines crop and shred the stalks. Heavy rollers extract the juice. Hissing evaporators thicken the juice to molasses. Whirling centrifugals separate the sugar crystals from the molasses. Then refining machinery washes, cleans, bleaches, and dries the crystals. In the last step, the sugar is packaged in cartons for the market.

Mechanized sugar cultivation is a far cry from those first Egyptian plantations. Today, newer and more productive varieties with thicker, juicier stalks are being developed by various governments, and there are experimental stations in Honolulu and in Queensland, Australia. Today, one harvesting machine can do the work of more than seventy-five laborers. And back-up irrigation systems, managed by computers, make sure that the ton of water that is needed to

Egyptian camels haul sugarcane to the mills, even as they did in the eighth century.
WFP/FAO photo

Harvesting sugarcane in Louisiana.   USDA–SCS photo

A highly improved experimental crop of sugarcane in Ceylon (with thicker stalks).
FAO photo

Sugarcane researchers in Ceylon inspect a very tall variety. *FAO photo*

produce each and every pound of sugar is supplied to the fields as required.

Besides serving mankind as an energy food, sugar is used in the manufacturing of such things as wallboard, plastics, varnish, and paper. Paper, however, is not made directly from sugar, but from the *bagasse*, that fibrous material that is left over after the juice is extracted from the stalks. Additionally, experimental tests show that automobiles can run on fuel derived from sugar. And, of course, rum is distilled from sugar.

Rum? It was the Spanish freebooters in Jamaica who noticed that the leftover molasses in the mill vats fermented quickly. That's how the first stills in the New World came to be. African slaves shoveled this fermented mash into homemade pot stills and heated it. At a certain temperature, the alcohol vaporized and was collected in a retort. When it condensed, it was powerful Jamaica rum, which found a ready market in Europe.

Today, rum is made all around the world, wherever that tall sweet grass, known botanically as *Saccharum officinarum*, is cultivated.

CHAPTER 9

The Forage Grasses

When cereal seeds are finely milled, sweetened with molasses, then cooked and served on plates—that's *food* for people. When the same seeds are coarsely ground, sweetened with molasses, then dumped into barn bins or feedlot troughs—that's *feed* for domesticated animals. Cornflakes and oatmeal eaten by people are food. Cracked corn and oats fed to hogs, poultry, and horses are feed.

In the minds of some, this feed should be rerouted to the cooking pots of the hungry in the developing countries. "Less feed for animals," they say, "would mean more food for people."

This statement is misleading. Worldwide, most domesticated animals are raised in fields and pastures, on grass that grows wild. They are less often fed grain. When grain is fed to animals (mostly hogs and poultry), it's of a lower quality than that consumed by people. And it's only in the affluent countries, where housewives can afford juicy, well-marbled cuts of meat, that cattle, sheep, hogs, and poultry are fed grain raised especially for them. However, the grain consumed by all the domesticated animals in the world amounts to no more than a very small percentage of the global harvest.

The practice of feeding heavy grain supplements to domesticated animals started during the 1950's. At that time, the United States was producing such great surpluses of wheat and corn that the price per bushel dropped drastically. Farmers and cattlemen, accordingly, took advantage of the low prices, and it became customary to fatten meat animals in feedlots on heavy supplementary feedings of grain. In turn, American housewives were taught to ask for "grain-fed" beef and lamb.

By the 1970's, however, as the global population soared, the grain market tightened. The price of wheat and corn skyrocketed and supplementary feedings of grain were reduced. By 1974, American beef cattle were once again spending most of their time on the ranges and consuming 82 percent of their feed in the form of *forage*.

Forage is made up of the leaves and stems of many different grasses, plus weeds and legumes. Animals graze on this forage in pastures and on ranges. In severe weather, they munch it in the form of hay or other stored crops, dropped to them by plane, or fed to them in snug barns.

Good forage is very nutritious. It contains sugar and starch, protein, vitamins, and cellulose. If only people could toss some forage into the cooking pot, they would not have to worry about food shortages. But this cannot be. People's stomachs cannot digest and absorb forage nutrients directly, but only after the *ruminants* process them into edible animal products.

Ruminants—sheep and goats, cattle and deer, as well as antelopes, giraffes, buffalo, and other grazing animals —have an extra stomach called the *rumen*. This extra stomach is inhabited by special microorganisms which act on the consumed forage in special ways. At an agricultural research station in Maryland, scientists can see this happening in a steer, which has a little window implanted in its side. They can see how the various grasses, weeds, and legumes are broken down for digestion. They can see how the coarse forages and some of the cellulose grass fibers pose no problem to the ruminant digestive system.

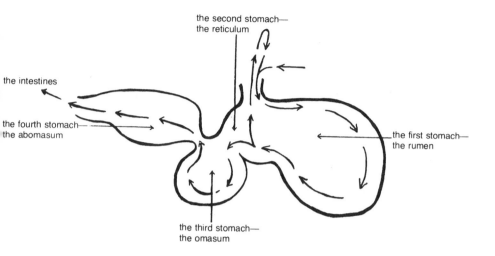

the second stomach—
the reticulum

the intestines

the fourth stomach—
the abomasum

the first stomach—
the rumen

the third stomach—
the omasum

Ruminants not only digest and metabolize these tough foodstuffs, they also *create* vast amounts of additional protein. They have this extraordinary ability to produce their own protein chemically from the carbohydrates and nitrogens in the various grasses they eat. This means that at the end of a day a ruminant has absorbed more protein from the grass than the grass had originally contained. This is an amazing and important ability, because, with it, the ruminants provide the rich protein base for man and other meat-eating animals. Take away this protein-building ability from the ruminants, and in the midst of the lushest grasslands, most of them would soon die of protein deficiency, because there isn't enough protein in grass to sustain them. The carnivores would fare even worse, because they can neither digest the forages nor produce protein from grass. Man, however, would manage to survive because he is omnivorous, but without beef, lamb chops, milk, or cheese, he would have to set quite a different table.

As it is, ruminants eat all day and consume enormous quantities of forage. They produce tremendous amounts of protein, which promotes growth and cell repair. They grow tremendously large. And they provide quantities of well-balanced protein foods that people *can* use in the cooking pot. Additionally, most of the world's domesticated ruminants graze most of their forage on the natural grazing lands. And note. Although these grazing lands contain much more acreage than all the available croplands put together, *they would not contribute to the human food supply if they were not grazed by the ruminants.* These lands are not suited to the intensive cultivation of cereal grain. They are either semiarid and thin-soiled, too steep or too stony, or completely under water during the tropical rainy seasons.

Those forage grasses which cover the drier plains, the steppes, and the savannas of the world consist of thousands of different species. Some are native grasses. Some have been transported and transplanted. And some have been greatly improved in the research laboratories.

In the United States, only about ten or twelve of these grasses provide most of the forage for the American herds. These grasses grow best in their own particular habitats: on the far-western Great Plains, the humid pastures of the North, the coastal areas, or the warm Southern states.

In the Congo, the native cattle naturally graze the native forages—molasses grass and guinea and tall stands of elephant grass. On the African veld, it is kikuyu and Rhodes grass that sustain them, while the Argentine cattle thrive on *Panicum* and bluegrass. In some countries (Panama, for instance), cattle are being grazed on improved pastures at experimental stations.

But no matter where the grazing areas may be, farmers who know how can produce as much as 400 pounds of beef a year from a well-managed acre of forage, on land that could not produce harvests of cereal grasses.

The worldwide need for animal protein and the worldwide shortage of good land has spurred scientific farmers to increase the size of their beef and dairy herds without increasing their acreage. For the beef herds, they concentrate on improving the grazing grasses. Using small air-

Big bluestem, a good sod former, thrives in forty-four states. A good pasture grass.
USDA–SCS photo

Little bluestem, more drought resistant than the big bluestem, thrives on the Great Plains.
USDA–SCS photo

Smooth brome, a leafy, sod-forming perennial that grows well in the corn states, in the Pacific Northwest, and Canada, survives periods of drought by becoming dormant.

USDA–SCS photo

planes, they seed the areas with suitable forage grass seeds and, using good management practices (meaning fertilizing, chemical dusting, and rotating), they produce high-quality grasses at the same time that they control the weeds. Such improved grasses are rich in carbohydrate content. They also contain more of the food value the ruminants need—A and D vitamins plus traces of such minerals as calcium, phosphorus, potassium, copper, cobalt, and common salt.

For obvious reasons dairy herds, which are raised primarily for their milk output, are grazed closer to home

A permanent brome pasture.   *USDA–SCS photo*

Timothy, a high-quality hay
plant, grows well in cool,
humid areas.
                    USDA–SCS photo

Alta fescue, a perennial bunchgrass—a high-quality forage grass, it is drought resistant but also grows well in humid areas.
USDA–SCS photo

than beef cattle on various kinds of pasture: (a) on hilly slopes or other poor lands, planted with selected perennial grasses; (b) on rotational pastures, planted with improved annual grasses and rotated every two or three years with other cultivated crops; (c) on supplemental pastures, meadows that after mowing are opened to the cattle for two or three months in the late summer and early fall, so they graze the *aftermath* (the stubble and the regrowth).

With all this forage growing on the grazing lands and in the pastures, there's still a feeding problem. Domesticated animals eat all year, but in most instances, the grasses don't grow all year. Most grasses are perennials, but each has its own growing season. Some come up early in the spring and die away in the summer. Some come up in summer, long after spring is gone. There are also autumn grasses, which replace the short-season summer grasses.

An Idaho pasture, permanently seeded to mountain brome.   *USDA–SCS photo*

And there are grasses that grow right through the winter, provided the frosts aren't too severe.

Many farmers have solved the problem of seasonal grasses. To extend the grazing season, they plant a mixture of good-quality grass seeds that will grow from early spring till late fall. Depending on the location, the mixture may contain timothy, bluegrass, or tall fescue for cool-season growth, plus bromegrass, orchard grass, and the Sudan grasses for late-spring and summer growth.

Planted or wild, these grasses, together with weeds and legumes, are feed for the ruminants, so it's foolish to quarrel with the practice of raising ruminant herds for meat and milk products, because the forage lands are not capable of producing cereal grass.

Livestock *may* be raised entirely on forage. The cattle will gain weight adequately and yield adequate amounts of milk. With supplementary grain feedings, however, they will produce *more* beef and *more* milk.

In the United States and some of the other Western countries, some grain is raised especially for supplementary feeding of farm animals. Or these same cereal grasses may serve as green forage in the fields, which the animals harvest for themselves. In the United States, livestock graze in fields of pearl millet, oats, and rye. In India and Australia, they graze Japanese millet. And in many depleted and outworn areas, animals graze in plantings of rye, which not only provides good winter feed but also holds the soil in place.

Still, much of the cereal grasses grown for supplementary animal feed are harvested by the farmers and stored away for those months when green grass is not available. Sometimes, corn, oats, and millet are harvested for their seeds. Other times, the whole plant may be stored away. Corn, for example, may be served to the animals as fodder—stalks, leaves, kernels, and cobs. More often it is prepared as *silage*.

In India—millet is grown for buffalo fodder.   *FAO photo*

When the corn is ready to be ensiled—when it is tall in the fields and ripe—the machines move in. The driver guides his tractor along the straight, yellowing rows. Behind him, drawn by the tractor, rumbles the harvester, a huge combine that severs the corn stalks close to the ground, then chops the entire plant into very fine pieces, and blows them into the forage truck.

Within minutes, the chopped-up corn is transferred from the truck to the silos, which are tall, cylindrical structures. There, after it is packed down to exclude the air, it begins to ferment and turn into still-green forage, called silage. Since fermentation enhances the feed value of the corn, farmers often add small amounts of molasses or nitrogen, urea or

Corn silos in Tennessee.   *USDA–SCS photo*

phosphorus to hasten the process. When winter winds whistle around the barn, this silage—succulent, tasty, and still green—is fed to the cattle.

In much the same manner, hay and pasture grasses are sometimes ensiled—cut, chopped, stored in airtight silos, and treated with chemical additives to encourage fermentation. Months later, the ensiled mixture, a highly nutritious feed, is forked by hand or by machine into the feeding troughs.

In the temperate zones, grass-filled silos are likely to contain mixtures of brome-, orchard, and fescue grasses. Or they may be filled with the new, fast growing hybrid Su-

Orchard grass for grass silos, Washington State.   *USDA–SCS photo*

dans and sorghum-Sudans. Sometimes, too, the silos may contain a mix of specially planted small grain grasses—oats and rye, wheat, barley, and millet.

In the tropics and subtropics, the silage mix is made up of grasses native to those regions—some of sugarcane, others of chopped guinea grass, still others of ribbon or tall elephant grass.

Hay, however, is the most important harvested forage crop, and it is made wherever year-round grazing is impossible because of the climate. Hay (which consists of wild or planted forage grasses) is first cut, then dried. It

Haymaking on a coastal Bermuda hay field in Georgia.   *USDA–SCS photo*

may be dried flat in the fields, on drying racks, or in specially heated structures. After drying, it is baled and stored in the barns, or if space there is lacking, the hay bales may be stacked on the fields and covered with a plastic sheet.

It is these cereal seeds bagged for the barn bins, these cereal grasses cultivated for the silos, and these bales of hay—all grown on good cropland—that trouble the grain-hungry people of the Third World. Although the world's cattle, sheep, and goats subsist almost entirely on forage, they still consume a fraction of the global grain harvest. It is a tiny fraction—no more than 1 or 2 percent—a fraction which is more than repaid by the animal products we derive from the livestock. (For meat contains the complete spectrum of the B vitamins which are needed for growth and for the prevention of mental retardation, and milk by itself is a near perfect food.) But to the hundreds of millions who are hungry, this 1 or 2 percent is cause for concern, because it comes out of man's cooking pot. As they say openly at the world food conferences, they find it hard to accept the fact that what is food for them is feed in the Western world. "How is it," they ask, "that sorghum is feed for cattle in the United States, but food for us, here in Africa?" Or "Why is corn, which is the dietary mainstay in Latin America and large parts of Asia and Africa, fed mostly to hogs and poultry in the United States?"

If the grain harvests continue to fall short of human needs, this concern may proliferate and erupt into trade wars. On the other hand, this concern may be considerably eased as research workers succeed in developing more productive and more nutritious forage grasses—grasses that grazing animals can harvest for themselves on the otherwise unproductive ranges. Such grasses would reduce the need to divert grain from the cooking pot to the feed bin. By boosting the production of meat and milk products, they would help to allay man's eternal hunger.

CHAPTER 10

Grass, Eternal Hunger, and History

Hunger is nothing new in the history of mankind. Early man spent most of his time hunting cereal seeds and edible game, yet he rarely accumulated a surplus. Consequently, he was eternally hungry.

There is evidence to suggest that this eternal hunger began to diminish about ten thousand years ago, shortly after the last Ice Age, when the human family began to change its lifestyle, on the grassy plains of the Fertile Crescent. The Fertile Crescent is that great curve of land which stretches from Egypt, through Palestine, into Mesopotamia, to the Persian Gulf. On those hot, subtropical plains, which are now dry and desolate, the soil was black and fertile. It was watered by two broad and muddy rivers, which flooded annually and left a rich coating of silt on the fields.

It was on those grassy plains that the human family became herder and farmer.

As herders, they drove their sheep and goats from field to farther field, where the grass was as yet ungrazed. With their possessions piled high on their snorting camels, with their wives and children straggling behind them, with their tents pitched at nightfall and guarded by sentries against jackals and hyenas, these nomads wandered for hundreds of miles every year. Their flocks multiplied till they numbered in the hundreds, the thousands, and even in the tens of thousands. By 5000 B.C., these herders were enjoying considerable prosperity, with annual surpluses of meat and butter and cheese salted away in goat-skin bags. But hunger had not really been banished from the world, for the grasslands, which they took for granted, were to be destroyed.

In the meantime, their cousins, the farmers, enjoyed similar prosperity. As the centuries passed, they learned to select the better seeds from their better cereal grasses. They learned to make wooden plows. They learned to channel the floodwaters to their plowed fields. They increased their harvests of emmer and bread wheat, barley and rye.

So great were the surpluses of grain and animal products, that the well-fed tribes of the Fertile Crescent were able to reduce their work force in the fields. The idled tribesmen soon learned to make hand tools and to build houses of brick made from the mud left by the annual floodings. They designed marketplaces where loin-clad laborers, laden with cheese and meat and pottery jars of grain, mingled with curly-bearded merchants, wearing long quilted skirts. They constructed temples and palaces and roads. They established schools for boys who, clay tablet and stylus in hand, learned reading and math, important skills for future traders and bookkeepers, bankers and real-estate brokers. They fashioned weapons for the military assigned to guard the royal residences, the trade routes, and the boundaries.

Magnificent cities and powerful empires arose in Mesopotamia, in Syria, in Lebanon, and in the Holy Land—civilizations that spread eastward to the lush grass-lands of China and westward to Egypt and beyond. As many as thirty empires arose on that Fertile Crescent in the past seven thousand years. These empires, abundantly provisioned with cereal grain and meat from the hinter-land, grew strong and mighty. But with few exceptions

(such as Babylon) they lasted only thirty or forty generations, sometimes sixty or seventy, no more. Some fell after
eight hundred years. Some survived for two thousand
years. All vanished, however, as their grasslands turned to
wastelands and could no longer grow grain for the people
or forage for their herds. Wastelands all, mighty cities like
Babylon and Kish were buried under drifting sands.
Others, like the Hundred Dead Cities of Syria, were abandoned in the desert, wind-whipped by swirling dust.

Reasons explaining the fall of these civilizations are
many: the disasters and the ravages of war . . . political
corruption and moral decay . . . a change in climate.

Ecologists and conservationists claim it was none of
these that created those barren wastelands. Such disasters
merely bring down governments and create untenable living conditions, they do not destroy civilizations. More-
over, geological studies indicate no significant changes in
climate in the Fertile Crescent. As for war, the Babylonians
were constantly embattled while building their empire, but
they recovered after each invasion and returned to their
grainfields and grazing grounds. Egypt was overrun and
conquered many times, but the Egyptians continued to
plant their rice, and Egypt did not vanish from the face of
the earth. And though historians claim that political
corruption and moral decay caused the fall of Rome, it was
rather the loss of "the Roman granary"—of the wheat fields
in North Africa—which ultimately brought about the
downfall of the civilization that was Rome.

According to experts in the field, it is the productivity of
the grasses that determines the continuance of a civilization. The grasses, as we have seen, are the food base for
man and his domesticated animals. As long as the grasses
grow abundantly, men find ways to build and rebuild a
troubled civilization. If, however, the grass cover is destroyed, then a disastrous environmental chain reaction
sets in.

If the grass cover is destroyed, the soil is exposed and
begins to move. In rainy weather, running water washes
away the soil particles. In scorching weather, the wind
blows them away and buries everything in its path. In

time, the soil is gone and only the subsoil—or, in some instances, the bare rock—is left. Then the watertable drops. The subsoil becomes parched and cracked. Since few plants can survive under such conditions, the region soon becomes barren. And the former fertile land, its cover of grass plants destroyed, is replaced by a wasteland.

In the Middle East, the grass cover was destroyed in the seventh century A.D., when hordes of Arabs swept out of the desert with great herds of sheep and goats. The sheep grazed the grass so closely that the leaves had no chance to grow back and became stunted and died. The goats did even more damage—they ripped up the plants, leaves, stems, roots, and all—till the grass cover was stripped away.

And so it came to pass that the grasslands of the Fertile Crescent were replaced by wastelands.

• Across the Jordan Valley is the Promised Land. Moses described it as "a land flowing with milk and honey" and "a land of wheat, and barley, and vines, and fig trees, and pomegranates." That was three thousand years ago. Now the ruins of Jericho tell another story—a story of a desolate

Excavated ruins of the city of Kish.   *USDA–SCS photo*

Hillside in Jordan, once covered with a layer of protective soil.   *USDA–SCS photo*

hinterland, where more than half of the red soil has been eroded, washed down from the hillsides and dumped on the lowlands.

• Syria, famous in biblical times for its wheat fields and splendid herds of cattle, is now dotted with wastelands. The city of Jerash, once home for 250,000 people, lies buried under thirteen feet of soil and gravel, which has been eroded from the surrounding hills. And yet, though the area is all desert now, the ancient water supply still operates. The same springs still bubble inside the masonry walls that were built by the local engineers in Greco-Roman times.

• Off to the north, in a man-made desert of one million acres, stand the Hundred Dead Cities of Syria. More like small market towns than full-sized cities, they stand exposed on the rolling hills, barren and empty. Once they were well supplied with meat and grain from the surrounding slopes and valleys, formerly grass covered.

• Farther to the south and westward lay the north coast of Africa, once the granary of Rome. In Caesar's time, the Roman cohorts used to complain about the heavy Tunisian rains that soaked the scattered trees of the natural savanna. Now the savanna is gone, and when the soaking rains fall, they fall only on the shifting sand, the gullied hills, and the buried cities.

Timgad is such a buried city. In the first century A.D., it was a great center of business and culture, with a public library, a forum, lavish Roman baths, a theater that seated 2,500, and marble toilets for the public. Timgad was surrounded by broad wheat fields. It was circled by hillside olive groves. In the seventh century A.D., it was overgrazed. Then land was eroded, and the city was buried under debris. Twelve hundred years later, it was excavated by French archaeologists.

Olive groves in Tunisia today, showing that the climate is still suitable for agriculture where the soil is still on the land.   *USDA–SCS photo*

A view of the former forested mountains (above Timgad). Erosion gouged the slopes.
USDA–SCS photo

Just as overgrazing can trigger an environmental chain reaction and turn a grassland into a desert wasteland, so, too, in the course of time, can a seemingly beneficent act of nature start another kind of chain reaction and create a similar wasteland.

On the Fertile Crescent, the flooding, muddy waters brought great benefits to the Baylonian grainfields. These waters carried minerals and nutrients and silt and humus in suspension, all the way from the eroded hills of Armenia, in the north. These waters fertilized the fields, nourished the planted cereal grasses, and created the civilization that was Babylon. But in the end, these life-giving waters destroyed Babylon, too.

The Babylonians, eager to boost their already abundant harvests, built a network of irrigation canals to control the floodwaters over ten thousand square miles of cropland. But the irrigation water, so beneficent, so life-giving, created two problems: It salted and it silted the fields.

In the absence of a good drainage system, the poured-on

irrigation water caused mineral salts to concentrate on the land. At the same time, the ever-present silt in the water clogged the canals and had to be shoveled out constantly by slaves. This shoveled-out silt was piled up along the embankments in mounds twenty to forty feet high.

The canals functioned quite successfully for some five thousand years. But when the Babylonians could no longer keep up with the endless shoveling, the irrigation system broke down, the plants withered, and the crops failed. Then the grain surpluses dwindled, the once-fertile fields faded to wasteland, and scarcity deepened to mass starvation. As Babylon died, it was buried under the shifting, windblown sands from the former grainfields.

So reads the ancient story of hunger in the Middle East. It begins with early man on the grasslands, eternally hunting for food. It proceeds through the time of early agriculture, with great herds grazing the forages and great stands of cereal grass growing on the irrigated plains. It moves on to the chain reaction of grassland destruction. And as the grasslands were abused by overgrazing and the grainfields were abused by salting and the deposition of silt, they turned into wastelands. And wastelands are not capable of producing cereal grass for man or forage for his domesticated animals.

Again and again, other lush grasslands were to beckon to the hungry. And the hungry, all unwittingly, were to abuse them to turn them into wastelands. This is what happened on the American prairies and Great Plains.

To the millions of hungry immigrants who crossed the Atlantic in the 1800's and headed for the Middle West and beyond, it seemed that the grasslands would last forever. And since their coming coincided with the coming of the Age of Science—the mechanization of farm equipment and the development of chemical fertilizers, herbicides, and pesticides—they did indeed produce great harvests.

By the 1900's, new machines were riding the prairies in double-quick tempo—stripping the sod, plowing, harrowing, and cultivating the cereal grasses. New farmers were harvesting unprecedented yields of grain. New herds of cattle and sheep by the millions were grazing the semiarid plains. And the galloping cowboy had become the counterpart of the ancient shepherd, wandering with his flock.

At the turn of the twentieth century, horses replaced the lumbering oxen between the shafts of farm machines, and again the production of grain, beef, mutton, and pork quickened. After World War I, when gas-powered farm machines began to replace the horses in the fields, production soared. Surely America's rich grasslands were capable of feeding the world. Surely the fertile American soil would, unlike the ancient lands of the Fertile Crescent, endure for more than a thousand generations.

A rich fertile American soil endured for all of two generations. Fifty years after 1880, the Great Plains were overgrazed. There was little grass cover left to feed the cattle or to protect the soil. By the 1930's, the rivers were running red, brown, yellow, and black with eroded soil. And in

In the United States—the effects of overgrazing on a slope.   *USDA–SCS photo*

Kansas and Oklahoma, heartland of the wheat country (and
of the new agricultural technology that stripped the sod
quickly and efficiently) the black prairie topsoil was
whirling away in the wind, blowing eastward, skimming
the Appalachian Mountains, darkening the sky above
Washington, and drifting two hundred miles out over the
blue Atlantic.

Here, in the New World, were the new American wastelands. Here was Babylon, Syria, Palestine, and Timgad all
over again.

And yet, the situation in the United States, although
equally hunger-producing, was quite different because this
was the Age of Science. The big question was, could science reclaim those wastelands, restore those grasslands,
and once again win the war against hunger?

In the United States, ten erosion-experiment stations
were set up to find out two things: 1. What caused the soil

In the United States—abandoned farmhouse, showing the disastrous effects of wind
erosion, 1937.   *USDA-SCS photo*

on the prairies to move—to wash away with the rain and blow away with the wind? 2. And how was this sort of washing and blowing to be prevented from happening again?

The experimental research showed that soil moved when there was little or no grass cover. At station after station, scientists found that fields planted to clean-tilled crops, such as cotton or corn, lost excessive amounts of soil because of *runoff*. (Runoff is the rainwater that doesn't soak into the fields but runs off into the ditches and streams.)

At the Clarinda, Iowa, Experimental Station (to cite just one example), an average field that was planted to corn lost twenty-five tons of soil a year. A similar field that was planted to Kentucky bluegrass lost only .3 ton during the same year. A projection, accordingly, shows the cornfield losing 7 inches of topsoil in forty-five years, by which time it would be almost totally unproductive. The grassed field,

Runoff from a cornfield, 1942.   *USDA–SCS photo*

however, would be holding up productively for something like three thousand years.

Such findings prompted the federal government to proceed in two directions, which were to serve as examples to other countries with similar problems. They set up a special program to help relaim the eroded grasslands. And they established the Soil Conservation Service, as a branch of the U.S. Department of Agriculture.

The farmers, with the aid of the government, the Conservation Service, and the Army Engineers, focused their efforts on keeping the soil in place.

On the dry, denuded, overgrazed Great Plains, they planted thousands of miles of trees, to break the force of the westerly winds.

On the rolling slopes of the prairies, they contoured the fields in alternating strips of corn and sod-forming grasses.

Contour stripping controls erosion, 1961. This field is contoured to strips of corn (a row crop) plus oats and millet.   *USDA–SCS photo*

Eighty acres of strip cropping, 1957—corn plus fescue plus lespedeza (a legume).
USDA–SCS photo

Corn was the money crop, but the grass strips soaked up the rain and prevented uncontrolled runoff from gouging gullies.

Also on the rolling slopes, they grassed the waterways with suitable grass plants to provide controlled drainage.

But a different approach was needed to reclaim the most seriously overgrazed lands, where even the native grasses would no longer grow. Plant explorers, sent out to find plants suitable for such damaged lands, returned with many varieties. These included (a) the short, hardy bunch-grass from southern Russia, which rooted and thrived on the hot and dusty prairies; (b) the crested wheatgrass from Turkestan, which soon covered the cool ranges of the North and Northwest; (c) the vigorous weeping love grass from East Africa, which was to spread throughout the drought-troubled Southwest; and (d) the native grama, buffalo, and bluestem grasses, whose growing habits had to be rediscovered by lab technicians. In short order, then, the Great Plains flushed green again with the native forages.

A grassed waterway planted to water-loving and water-tolerant grasses, 1955.
USDA–SCS photo

Crested wheat from Turkes-
tan now covers the cool
ranges of the North and
Northwest in the United
States.
USDA–SCS photo

Weeping love grass, a perennial from east Africa, now thriving in the drought-troubled Southwest in the United States.   *USDA–SCS photo*

By the 1950's, America's reclaimed grasslands were producing such surpluses of grain as the world had never seen.

But nothing lasts forever. By the midsixties, the grain surpluses were decreasing rapidly, because the world population was increasing at an alarming rate. By the seventies, global shortfalls, due to poor weather and poorer harvests, red-inked the worldwide shortage of grain and the increasing evidence of hunger in the Third World.

Stung by these shortages, the scientists turned to the research and came up with the concept that grass is not just an end product of grassland agriculture, but a total system. Grass improves the soil and prevents erosion both underground, by way of its roots, and topside, by way of its stems and leaves.

Underground, grass roots anchor the plant to the soil, so that neither plant nor soil can blow away in the wind.

Pushing downward, the roots make the soil porous. This permits air and water to percolate through. Every year, tons of roots—as much as one to ten tons of dry weight —are produced by grass plants on just one acre of ground. Since one third of these roots die off annually, they enrich the soil with that much organic material.

Topside, the grass leaves do more than furnish food for grazing animals. The long pliant leaves can also protect the ground from the searing heat of the summer sun, from killing frosts, and from the hard, beating action of the raindrops.

Raindrops often pelt the ground with tremendous force. Scientists theorize that one inch of rain, falling on one acre

The roots of one perennial grass plant—an impressive amount. *USDA-SCS photo*

Grass plants, like the blue grama on the left, have elaborate root systems that effectively hold the soil in place. But if the area is overgrazed, lesser plants, like the one on the right, move in. These lesser plants have different root systems, which are not effective in holding the soil in place.   *USDA–SCS photo*

of ground, contains enough energy to lift that acre (if it were seven inches thick) to a height of one foot. So great is the force of these raindrops—so tightly do they pack the soil particles, so hard do they slick the surface of the soil —that a bare field may become virtually waterproof. On such a bare field, the soil becomes incapable of absorbing the falling rain, and the water can only run off in gully-gouging torrents.

It was grassland agriculture as a total system that created the great surpluses of grain and animal products in the 1950's and 1960's and, to a degree, eased man's eternal hunger. But there are still millions of eroding acres in the United States, in other Western countries, and increasingly in the less-developed countries.

Given the exploding populations and the grain shortfalls, who can deny that these eroding grasslands, with their diminished capacity for production, serve only to *aggravate* man's problem of eternal hunger?

CHAPTER 11
Malthus, Math, and the Limits of Growth

The earth we live on may be heading into the twenty-first century as a hungry planet. Although the grazing herds are larger than ever, and the yield of cereal grain and animal feed is greater than ever, the rate of increase in global food production has not kept pace with the rate of increase in global population. There is not enough grain and there are not enough animal products to meet the world demand now—and the global population is still rising.

Of course, population has been increasing since the time of the cavemen. In those days, however, the death rate was high and life expectancy low. A young father, foraging for food, as often as not became food for other animals. The mothers, as well as the children playing near the cave, often suffered the same fate.

Population increased so slowly that it had barely reached the quarter-billion mark by the time Christ was born. Then it took 1,600 years to double that, to people the earth with half a billion. The next doubling took only 230 years so that, by 1830, when the European immigrants were settling the American prairies, world population topped a billion.

Within the next century, with the Age of Science on hand, grain growing became more productive. This expanded productivity provided the resources for an increased population. Larger families, with many sons and daughters living in large farmhouses, became customary, and many grandparents lived to a ripe old age. In turn, this increased population pressure provided the incentive to increase productivity still more—to extend the grainfields, buy more combines, and increase the size of the herds.

By 1930, global population had again doubled, and numbered two billion. Thirty-four years later, in 1964, there were three billion people.

By 1976, when four billion were inhabiting Planet Earth, the population–production race had become decidedly uneven. Where there had been grain surpluses, there were now deficits, accompanied by the threat of world famine.

"Why don't the farmers produce more grain? Increase their acreage? Double their harvests?"

The Western world has more than once doubled its production of grain, but the global population increased faster. Even though the yields of wheat, rice, and corn on experimental plots have increased manyfold, such yields are not automatically guaranteed for open fields, for a very good reason. Soil and water and climate cannot be controlled so easily on the open fields as on experimental plots. And aside from the fact that cropland is limited, many once highly productive areas of the world have been worn out. The wastelands around Babylon and Kish and Jerash are stark reminders. In southwest Asia, too, lands which supported great rice-eating populations for thousands of years have become so depleted and eroded they can no longer feed a similar population. Additionally, formerly good croplands in Cambodia and Vietnam have been blasted by military machines, poisoned by defoliants, and deliberately turned into wastelands.

This adds up to a population–food imbalance, a situation that is further aggravated by the fact that you can always count on people's appetites, but you can't always count on the harvests. Even on the most scientifically tended grainfields, harvests are sometimes chancy. Late frosts may kill early plantings; torrential rains may wash out the fields; prolonged droughts may wither the seedlings; and new strains of insects or viruses, resistant to all known insecticides and fungicides, may destroy the plants before they can form seed heads.

Actually, the population–food imbalance is not new. It was recognized as long ago as 1798 by the Reverend Thomas Robert Malthus, a British economist. Arguing that population tends to outstrip the food supply, Malthus warned of a worldwide population–food imbalance. He was immediatёly called a prophet of doom because good, arable land was plentiful and the global population stood at a low 700 million. In 1798, who could imagine a population of five, six, or eight billion, two hundred years later?

Malthus foresaw these food shortages because he was an economist and noted that population tends to increase *geometrically*, while food production increases *arithmetically*. (A geometric progression increases by a fixed *multiple*, as for example, *times* 2. An arithmetic progression, on the other hand, increases by a fixed *difference*, as for example, *plus* 2.)

To consider the geometric increase, assume that families will produce, on the average, four children, who will live and marry and in turn also produce families of four children. If we start with two couples and eight children in the first generation, we will have sixty-four couples producing 256 children by the sixth generation, some 150 years later. And here is how this computation works out:

GENERATION	COUPLES	CHILDREN PRODUCED
1	2	8 children who will form 4 couples
2	4	16 children who will form 8 couples
3	8	32 children who will form 16 couples
4	16	64 children who will form 32 couples
5	32	128 children who will form 64 couples
6	64	256 children who will form 128 couples

Now consider the matter of food production, which increases arithmetically. The original two couples, together with their eight children, lived on a piece of land that produced just enough to feed them adequately. With proper agricultural practices, this land can be made to double its productivity and possibly double it again. But to feed 256 children, some 150 years later, the original land would have had to become thirty-two times more productive—or those children would have had to acquire thirty-two times more land.

No one, so far, knows how to multiply productivity, *on a global scale,* thirty-two times, or even ten times. And no one as yet knows how to find additional cropland that, with our present technology, can be cultivated economically. A case in point is central and southern Africa, where farmers and herders are locked out of 2.8 million square miles of potentially good land (this is five times the area farmed in the United States) by the tsetse fly and its scourge of sleeping sickness.

During the twentieth century, serious population–food imbalances became noticeable because of the soaring birthrate and the declining death rate. Accordingly, a number of countries tried to find solutions.

Some set up family-planning councils in the hope of reducing population growth. In the less-developed countries, however, the idea of such planning was thought by many to be a form of genocide. Their population, consequently, continued to rise at an astronomical rate.

Elsewhere, in the hope of increasing the production of grain and livestock, some governments established grassland improvement programs: England and Wales focused on rotating seeded sheep pastures and grainfields. The Netherlands established pilot farms to demonstrate the ways by which grass roots improve the soil. Australia used the harvested wheat fields as winter pasture. And large tracts of the Algerian steppes, where droughts occur periodically, were set aside as fodder preserves for sheep.

Other countries pushed grassland improvement programs along similar lines: In Argentina, the commission devised a seasonal seeded pasture calendar for grazing grass. In Kenya, with three fourths of the land suited mainly for grazing, farm schools trained students in scientific cattle raising.

These grassland programs were not too effective. They were insufficiently funded, they could not be enforced, and they had little impact on the global harvests.

By 1970, grain shortages loomed so large in the less-developed countries because the population-growth curve had thrown the flow of grain into reverse.

In the years before World War II, the less-developed countries, with two thirds of the world's population contained within their borders, were great *exporters* of grain. Two or three decades later, these same countries, currently comprising three fourths of the world's population, have become great *importers* of grain.

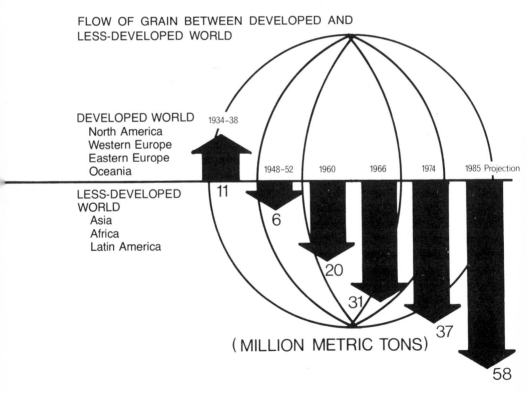

FLOW OF GRAIN BETWEEN DEVELOPED AND LESS-DEVELOPED WORLD

DEVELOPED WORLD
North America
Western Europe
Eastern Europe
Oceania

LESS-DEVELOPED WORLD
Asia
Africa
Latin America

1934–38

11

1948–52   1960   1966   1974   1985 Projection

6

20

31

37

(MILLION METRIC TONS)

58

The global situation worsened as reports of grain short-falls started coming in from some of the Western and Latin American countries. At the same time, rising affluence around the world began to drain off some of the world's food supply. In Europe and South America, Australia, Ethiopia, Nigeria, Egypt, and the Far East, mothers increasingly abandoned the practice of breast feeding and demanded baby bottles and cow's milk. It was a status symbol! Equally explosive was the demand for grain-fed beef and other highly nutritious animal products. In Japan, for example, you can easily see the effect of this affluence. Japanese children are so much taller and sturdier than their parents that they require larger seats and desks in the classrooms.

But haven't great increases been realized on the wheat fields of Mexico, the United States, Canada, and the Soviet Union? Haven't rice and corn crops topped all known harvests since the beginning of history?

The answer to both of these questions is yes. More food has been produced. But if the grain crop was great, the baby crop was greater. And the developing countries often couldn't afford to buy what food was available.

There were no bargains anywhere—not in cereal grain and not in additional grasslands. Although still higher yields *were* scientifically possible, such yields carried a price tag. They required more energy, more chemicals, and more machinery, as well as a good distribution system. These things cost more money than anyone could spend. The math of the situation was indisputable.

Hunger is a great motivater. By the midseventies, it had toppled some fifteen or twenty governments. That was because some 225,000 additional mouths were coming to breakfast every morning. That's because the world's population was increasing by 225,000 persons per day.

Under the stress of augmented populations and insufficient grain production, the doomsday predictions of Malthus were reactivated. Was Malthus correct when he stated that food production increases arithmetically, while population increases geometrically *unless* it's checked (by a high death rate or a low birthrate)?

Those who claim that Malthus was wrong point to our superior agricultural technology and the fact that there's plenty of unused land that could be planted to cereal grass. They urge the development of millions of unused marginal acres—the deserts, the high plains and the steppes, the mountain slopes, the coastal marshes, and the mighty sun-drenched river valleys in the tropics.

According to the enthusiastic anti-Malthusians, these acres could be put to the plow and made to produce, magnificently. They also suggest melting the North Polar glaciers, after which the land could be planted to the new, quick-growing cereal grasses. They look at all this unused marginal land and see solutions to the problem of feeding four billion people—or forty or fifty or even sixty billion.

Those who believe that Malthus was right—that population, unchecked, would indeed outstrip food production—even these people agree that the marginal lands could be made to grow cereal grasses abundantly. But they indicate two major deterrents to the development of such lands. One is economic, the other is environmental.

Economics means money. The pro-Malthus people point out that with enough money for agricultural inputs and energy, cereal grasses could be grown on the moon; with enough money, scientific agriculturalists could irrigate the deserts, regulate the global water supply, and control the temperature on the growing fields. But the cost of the cereals grown on such developed lands would be prohibitive—uneconomic. A loaf of wheat bread, a pound of rice, or a dozen ears of corn would be beyond the reach of all but the very rich.

Then there's the environmental trap, which is built into every proposal that calls for a restructured environment. Take the development of the deserts, for instance. Deserts need only water "to bloom like a rose." There's plenty of ancient fossil water in the vast subterranean reservoirs, and it's available for irrigation purposes. But subterranean water is a consumable resource. In some areas, it would be used up within a decade, or two or three, just as it is being used up now in Mexico City (where, because the water table keeps dropping, the city keeps sinking) and in the

American Southwest, where the water table drops ten feet a year. As Georg Borgstrom, distinguished author and expert on food science and geography, points out, modern agriculture requires tremendous quantities of water. It takes three hundred gallons to produce a loaf of bread and 3,500 gallons to produce a one-pound steak.

Of course, water could be obtained from the ocean, but extensive desalinization creates other problems. The extracted salt would have to pile up somewhere. In time, this piled-up salt would contaminate the soil along the coast and turn the surrounding waters into dead seas. Additionally, massive amounts of energy would be required to carry the desalinated water from the coast a thousand miles inland, and that would also cost money.

Or take the development of the semiarid ranges and the mountain slopes. Plowed and planted to grain, the thin soil there would soon blow away in the wind, and the rain would wash mud floods into the valleys—a grim picture, reminiscent of the American Dust Bowl in the 1930's and of the happenings in Syria and Timgad millennia ago.

Or take the draining of the marshes. If the coastal marshes were drained, the salty sea, unchecked by the solid presence of marsh water, would seep inland and kill the crops. It would also (as has happened in some parts of Florida) seep farther inland and contaminate the supply of drinking water.

Or take the great tropical river valleys—case in point, the Amazon River basin. Nearly 95 percent of the Amazon lands are underwater during the rainy season. The remaining 5 percent aren't trouble free, either. The soil is thoroughly leached and very rancid. It contains very little in the way of minerals and even less of organic materials. It is plagued with ground fungus, because there are no seasonal frosts to kill off the fungi. It is so overrun with ants and termites that few plants and animals can survive on the ground. Even chickens and other small domesticated creatures have to be suspended in cages and hung from the trees.

And finally, take the polar ice. The proposal to melt the glaciers and bring the Arctic region into grassland production sounds good—but there's the matter of meltwater. Since the meltwater would have to go someplace, it's logical to assume it would drain into the sea. Some scientists believe that this enormous amount of water would raise the sea level nearly two hundred feet around the world, inundating the coastal cities and destroying them.

These are some of the problems that could be expected to accompany extensive worldwide development of the marginal lands. But these problems need not surface—not if solid conservation practices are followed on the farms and if the marginal lands are only minimally developed and used as forage preserves.

Almost two hundred years ago, Malthus, operating on mathematical probabilities, predicted a population–food imbalance—the kind we are presently experiencing. Many disagreed with that prediction then, even as many disagree with that prediction now, believing there is no limit to the number of people who could inhabit the earth and no limit to the amount of cereal grass the earth could produce.

Today, however, computer printouts further Malthus' prediction. At the Massachusetts Institute of Technology, the First World Computer indicates that *the earth's natural limits of growth* in food production and population density will be reached within the next century.

Other dire predictions conjure up runaway disaster, fueled by massive famines. But these are not guaranteed predictions! Present trends (in population, industrialization, pollution, and the depletion of natural resources) may be replaced by other trends and other possibilities. Widespread famines and nuclear wars may increase the death rate. Determined family planning may decrease the birthrate. New economical sources of energy may boost grain production to unbelievable yields. New biological techniques and new agricultural technologies may make it possible to produce high yields at a price that's right. Weather modification may make it possible to control those yields.

These are some of the trends and some of the possibilities that may turn the population-food imbalance around. But these trends and these possibilities cannot be guaranteed any more than the dire predictions of Malthus can be guaranteed.

What about the future? What about the limits of growth? What about the grain shortfalls and the conquest of hunger? And what about the increasing population that needs more food *now*?

The United Nations, the various national governments, the World Bank, the international religious organizations, the conservationists, the ecologists, and the Joe Blows in the street—all offer plans and urge preparation for a viable and humane future for all of mankind. But what plans? What preparation?

Ken Boulding, noted economist, has one answer to these questions. "The way to prepare for the future," he said, "is to prepare to be surprised—because you surely will be."

In the meantime, grass scientists are proposing some surprising solutions to hunger, through continued and accelerated research in plant breeding and improvement.

CHAPTER 12

Grass for the Conquest of Hunger

By the FAO's most conservative estimate, 500 million people on earth are starving or severely malnourished. This figure is equivalent to the world's total population in the year 1630. In good times, when the crops grow well, these 500 million consume per capita four hundred pounds of grain a year. That's more than a pound a day of rice or corn, millet or sorghum.

Even if the global population were to remain at zero growth, greater grain harvests would be needed, and for that, three questions have to be answered: 1. How can the farmers produce more of the cereal grasses? 2. How can they make each of these grasses produce more seeds? 3. How can they make sure of the harvests?

The answers come from all directions—from the engineers and the chemists, the agricultural technicians, the geneticists, and the global housekeepers. And it could be that these answers, implemented and directed by a world body, just might conquer the eternal problem of hunger.

• The engineers, peering through their transits and busy with their blueprints, say the answer to increased grain

116

production lies in more dams, more reservoirs (for hydro-electric power and irrigation), and in more underground water cisterns. "Give the fields sufficient water, and you'll not have to worry about the harvests." They also point out that with enough water, multiple crops are possible in the subtropics. There are, however, a number of factors built into these engineering projects that negate their value in the fight to increase long-range productivity of the cereal grasses.

The great American grain surpluses of the 1950's and 1960's resulted, in part, from the great engineering projects of the 1930's—the thousands of dams and irrigation systems built after the Dust Bowl years. In the same way, dams and reservoirs in the Third World (funded by the United Nations, the United States, the Soviet Union, and

Lake Ballinger Dam in Texas.   *USDA–SCS photo*

Lake Ballinger Dam reservoir filled up and abandoned.   *USDA–SCS photo*

other nations) have provided water and hydroelectric power to millions of acres of formerly unproductive cropland.

But a dam or an irrigation system is not the last word in the fight to conquer hunger.

Build a dam, and the reservoir fills up with silt and sand in about thirty years, after which it has to be abandoned. And the silting basins, which are now constructed along with the newer dams, also fill up and have to be shoveled out periodically, or abandoned.

Irrigation systems, on the other hand, have a way of destroying the productivity of the land by creating drainage problems. In some instances, the irrigation water may waterlog the soil, taint it with mineral salts, and make it unfit for cultivation. This has happened in parts of the

A reservoir being filled up in Spartanburg, South Carolina.   *USDA—SCS photo*

In California—concentration of soluble salts. Soil may be reclaimed by leaching, improved drainage, and controlled irrigation.   *USDA—SCS photo*

United States, Pakistan, and elsewhere. Although such soils may be reclaimed by leaching, by improved drainage, and controlled irrigation, the expense is enormous.

• White-coated chemists insist it's the agricultural chemicals that boost productivity. "Additional nitrogen fertilizer," they say, "actually substitutes for additional land, since one well-fertilized acre produces as much or more grain as two, three, or four unfertilized acres." They also observe that certain agricultural chemicals spell death to weeds, molds, insects, and plant diseases.

• Technicians urge the development of appropriate intermediate agricultural technology for the less-developed countries, instead of the Western-style power-driven combines. Intermediate agricultural machines must be simple enough to be manufactured and repaired locally. They must be inexpensive so that the natives of less-developed countries can afford to buy them. They must be light in weight so that a man is able to lift them at the end of a tilled row. Land is so precious in these countries that farmers cannot afford to leave any of it unplanted so the machine can be turned around.

Intermediate technology—a hand-drawn rice seeder, Philippines.   *IRRI photo*

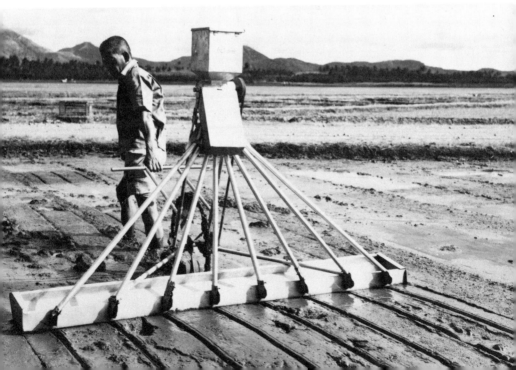

Intermediate technology—a new table thresher, Philippines.   *IRRI photo*

Agricultural technicians see these intermediate machines as the lever that will break the production impasse. They call attention to the seeders that can plant pregerminated rice seeds twenty to twenty-five times faster than a hand sower, and to the small rotary weeders that are five times faster than push-type weeders and eight times faster than manual weeding. They decry the use of draft animals, which work only part of the year but have to be fed all year around.

• Now plant geneticists, plant breeders who work with *hybrids* and *genes*, have learned how to develop new plants according to specification. These are man-made hybrids, cultivated on experimental test plots.

A hybrid is a new kind of plant grown from a seed which was the result of cross-pollination—the male pollen grains from one parent plant were deposited on the female pistil of a different parent plant. Seeds resulting from such cross-pollination grow into hybrid plants that are quite different from either of their parents because they carry the genes of both plants.

Genes are units of heredity, which carry heritable traits.

Intermediate technology—a rotary tiller, Philippines.   *IRRI photo*

In the Philippines—traditional plowing behind caraba.   *IRRI photo*

They may be traits of size and color and texture. They may be traits of immunity. They may be traits with a built-in resistance to frost or drought or disease. Hybrids, consequently, are full of genetic surprises—some good, some bad, some hopeless. Those twelve-inch ears of corn on the roadside stands, and that beautiful, high-yielding corn now growing in India, carry the genes for yellow color and long, slim cobs. If, additionally, they are delicious, they carry a desirable taste gene.

In nature, hybrids often occur at random. The story of how these man-made hybrids were developed started long ago. The first plant developers were the barefoot farmers of the Fertile Crescent, who every year selected the best seeds of their best emmer and bread wheats, barleys, and ryes for the next year's planting.

In India—a woman who is trained in modern methods raises an excellent crop of corn.
FAO photo

Seven thousand years later, the prairie farmers on the American cornfields were still using the selection method of crop improvement. Within a hundred years, however, farmers everywhere were to be astonished by the spectacular twentieth-century high-yielding hybrid corn and by the new science of genetic engineering, which was right around the corner.

Today, whether it's wheat that's being hybridized at the CIMMYT Center in Mexico or tropical corn at the CIAT Center in Colombia or rice at the International Rice Research Institute in the Philippines, the approach, the method, and the process are basically the same. And the aim is the same—to increase the yield for the conquest of hunger. But the science had its beginnings in the American corn belt in the nineteenth century with the "corn cranks."

For sixty years, Jake Leming tramped his Ohio cornfields, which had originally been planted to black-kerneled, late-maturing Indian corn. Selecting, always selecting, he consistently chose his seed corn from the early-ripening plants with the longest ears and the lighter, more attractive kernels. And in 1878, the long, beautiful, completely golden, early-ripening Leming corn was yielding a hundred bushels to the acre. It was unprecedented yield, and it won the Grand Prix at the Paris World's Fair.

In Central Illinois, long-bearded Jim Reid stumbled onto a natural high-yielding hybrid. His father had planted a few bushels of good old Ohio corn. But the planting was rained out, and the spaces had to be replanted with a local variety called Indian Yellow. Reid planned to select the best ears for seed corn—if there were any good ones. The new ears (progeny of the two varieties, which had been cross-pollinated in the field) were more beautiful than either the Ohio parent or the Indian parent. They were yellower. They were studded with keystone-shaped kernels, each with a little dent in the middle. They were longer and heavier yielding. Year after year, Jim planted his Yellow Dent, and he won so many prizes that farmers from a hundred miles around rode in to fill their saddle bags with Reid's Yellow Dent seed corn—as much as they could afford at $150 a bushel.

Not everybody, however, who planted the Leming or the

Reid corn got the same good results after the first year. Was this the fault of the farmers' methods or of the seeds which had been selected for beauty and yield?

James Beal, a professor at a small Michigan agricultural college, had been wondering about that and thought he knew the reason for those undependable harvests. The kernels on a single ear (he explained to anyone who would listen) are formed by two parents: by the ovules in the female pistils, all of which carry the female genes, and by the male pollen, blowing in a golden haze from the hundreds of different corn plants—blowing and landing on the sticky silks that led to the pistils. A single ear of corn, according to Beal, was like a horticultural racial mix of "half-

In Outer Mongolia—corn plant shows male tassels and female silks.   *FAO photo*

sisters"—father unknown. Corn seeds, he argued, could not be pedigreed by the selection method. Still, he gave the farmers one helpful suggestion. "Go through your fields at tasseling time," he said. "Identify the shabby, miserable-looking plants. Jerk off their tassels before they have a chance to produce pollen grains. In this way, your young ear shoots will be denied the male pollen of your inferior plants."

George Shull, who worked at the Evolution Lab in Cold Spring Harbor, carried this thinking a bit further. He reasoned that a single kernel of local corn carried innumerable ancestral traits (some good and some bad), passed down from corn that may have flourished on the mountains of Peru, the arid Southwest, and/or the stony fields of New England. If only he could isolate particular desirable traits!

Shull decided to try to do just that. He decided to bypass the selection method. He would become a plant breeder, and *inbreed* till he developed pure corn strains. And with this decision, Shull took a giant step toward the creation of man-made hybrids.

Inbreeding—breeding a corn plant to itself—is just a matter of forcing the plant to pollinate itself. So he planted some corn seeds and, at the proper time, fastened paper bags over the tassels before the pollen was produced and over the ear shoots before the silks were produced. After the pollen ripened, he shook the grains onto the same plant's sticky silks. In this way, he made sure that the new seeds that were to develop on the cobs would be the progeny of the *one* corn plant—and would, consequently, carry the genes of the one parent plant. Shull repeated this process a number of times, and by the fourth generation, his seeds were breeding true.

Shull's inbreds were pure, all right, but they were pure dwarf and pure spindlies, pure scragglies and pure low-yields. So then he did what nature does all the time. He crossbred—but under controlled conditions. He planted two of his inbred varieties, a stunted dwarf and a tall spindly. The ripened dwarf ears he saved for seed corn. And the following summer, what a surprise! What a splendid man-made hybrid! The plants were tall, vigorous, and

A worker in Columbia uses Shull's paper-bag method to control pollination of a corn plant. *Courtesy The Rockefeller Foundation*

sturdy. The yield? A record crop—a classic example of hybrid vigor.

Spurred on by Shull's success, plant breeders went to work to create their own corn hybrids in the research labs of the USDA, in the agricultural colleges, and at small seed farms. Thousands of trials later, and thousands of inbreds and crossbreds later, they achieved what they were after —the modern, delicious, high-yielding corn hybrid. It had larger ears. It had fuller kernels. It was adapted to grow in the rich, black soil of the American prairies.

Again and again, the breeders crossed this hybrid corn with other pure strains till they developed hybrids that were especially suited for growing in different areas and under different conditions. Drought resistance was bred into varieties slated for the old Dust Bowl. Quick maturation was bred into varieties destined for the northern states where the growing season is short.

These hybrid corns produced magnificently. And the 1940 average of forty-six bushels per acre rose to ninety-seven in 1972—and on one well-managed farm to a record 306 bushels per acre in 1975. One problem remains, and a vexing one it is, especially to the poor in the less-developed countries. Hybrid corn, like all hybrids, breeds true only once. Consequently, it produced a dependable, pedigreed crop only once. American farmers as well as farmers all over the world have to buy their hybrid seeds from specialized seed companies every year.

On a global scale, and by the way of an international effort, the big breakthrough in restructuring the various cereal grasses came about in the 1960's. Around the world, research centers, funded by the United Nations, the World Bank, thirteen governments, and a number of private foundations were set up and/or expanded. This time the search was on for high-yielding hybrids that would be so tailored and so structured that they would be able to thrive

A Moroccan farmer discusses his hybrid corn with a government worker.
FAO photo

over vast areas and under varying conditions of temperature, latitude, elevation, and rainfall.

At the CIMMYT Center in Mexico, work proceeded in much the same way. ("CIMMYT" is the Spanish acronym for International Maize and Wheat Improvement.) Here, *the* name is Norman Borlaug. The biggest hunger fighter of them all, Borlaug won the 1970 Nobel Peace Prize for his development of the Mexican dwarf wheats. Sponsored by the Rockefeller Foundation, he went to Mexico in 1944 to help improve the farming practices in that hungry land. And what a formidable job that was, because Mexican agriculture had not changed for two thousand years. The crops were still being harvested with a hand sickle, and the national average in wheat production was twelve bushels per acre.

Improving the wheat yield took first priority, but the wheats were plagued by a fungus disease called rust. At harvest time, the rust spores blew in reddish-brown clouds and settled on the fields for miles around. They shriveled the wheat and reduced the harvests, sometimes to 50 percent, other times to zero.

There were countless wheat varieties, all supposedly derived from a handful of seeds mixed in with a cargo of rice that had come with Cortez in 1519. But of all the varieties, Borlaug found only two that were resistant to rust. These two, however, were low yielding and, if treated with fertilizer, simply grew taller and leafier, without producing more grain.

Thirteen years and thousands of crosses later, Borlaug had the rust problem licked and the Mexican wheats, though still low yielding, could be relied on to grow into harvests. At that point, he crossed some of his rust-free wheats with a wheat plant that had been derived from a short, stiff-strawed Japanese variety, and the new Mexican dwarf hybrids made history in a hungry world. This hybrid absorbed fertilizer prodigiously and just as prodigiously produced heavy seed heads, yielding, on well-managed farms, as much as 105 bushels per acre. Those dwarfs were so stiff-stemmed that they could support their heavy seed heads. They were so short that they didn't lodge—that is,

A wheat field in Iraq, showing Mexican wheats that are resistant to lodging.

FAO photo

topple over in the rain. And, since the *photoinsensitivity* gene had been bred in, those wheats were no longer sensitive to day length. They could grow in the tropics as easily as in the subtropics. They could ripen quickly in the spring when the days were getting longer, and just as quickly in the fall when the days were getting shorter. They could produce two crops a year!

By the 1960's, despite a rapidly rising population, Mexico had become self-sufficient in wheat production and was supplying millions of tons of "miracle" wheat seeds to impoverished, less-developed countries. By the late 1960's, accordingly, India and Pakistan had also become self-sufficient in wheat production.

All eyes being on Borlaug and his Mexican dwarf wheats, the IRRI (the International Rice Research Institute) was set up in the Philippines, to do for rice what Borlaug

Wheat breeding in Baghdad, Iraq.   *FAO photo*

had done for the wheats—to create rice hybrids that were good tasting and rugged enough to grow abundantly just about anywhere in the warm regions.

They turned first to various seed banks. Seed banks, also called germ plasm banks, are worldwide collections of refrigerated cereal seeds, which are housed in the research centers. At these centers, trained seed specialists first select the most promising of the local cereal grasses, analyze them, and check out their limitations. After that, they follow the now standard techniques of inbreeding and crossbreeding these native varieties with seeds selected from the seed banks.

For continued vigor, the plant breeders recross their developed hybrids with some of the primitive strains, which are fast disappearing from the fields.

The breeders at IRRI started with a high-yielding tropical

semidwarf rice from Taiwan, a variety that was not at all popular because of its poor taste quality. This semidwarf they crossed with a tall, disease-resistant rice plant from Indo-China, and with other varieties from the seed bank.

Thirty-eight crosses and three years later, the new rice hybrids IR5 and IR8 appeared on the market, followed by IR20, with its improved grain quality. These rice hybrids were dwarfed so they wouldn't topple into the paddies during the monsoons. Their stems were stiffened so they could absorb more fertilizer and support heavier seed heads. And their leaves were redesigned, bred shorter and

In India—new rice strain produces five hundred grains per seed head, compared to 180 grains produced by traditional seed head.   *FAO photo*

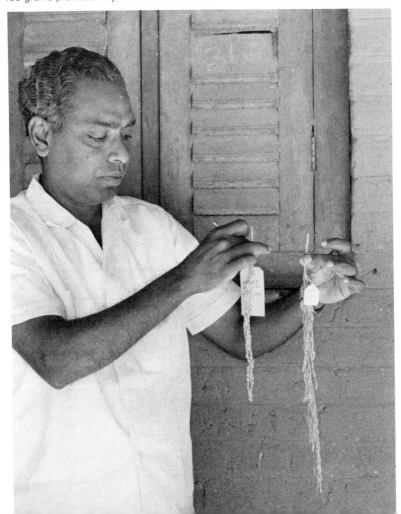

In India—farmers are shown the merits of the new Jaya rice in the field.
Courtesy The Rockefeller Foundation

more vertical so they could soak up more sunlight and permit the plants to grow closer together—an important factor where paddies are small and land is at a premium. Additionally, the photoinsensitivity gene was bred in so that these rice dwarfs (like the wheat dwarfs) could grow over a wider latitude. And then—the growing season was altered. It was cut down from the traditional 160 days to 100 days. And this permitted the farmers to raise three crops a year in the same old paddies.

At CIAT (the Spanish acronym for the International Center for Tropical Agriculture in Colombia) the research specialists restructured the corn plant to meet the needs of the Latin Americans and of those Africans and Asians who subsist on corn. They started with the local, luxuriant corn variety, which was about twenty feet tall but produced only a few tiny ears, set high on the stalk. They inbred and

IR8 rice being grown by a tenant farmer in Luzon, Philippines.   *AID photo*

crossbred this lanky specimen till they achieved a shorter hybrid. It was a disease-resistant hybrid, studded with high-yielding ears. It did nothing, however, for the "hidden hunger" plaguing the poor who lived mainly on corn. This hidden hunger stems from a lack of balanced protein, the kind that promotes growth and well-being. In West Africa, for example, it takes the form of a dreaded deficiency disease, called kwashiorkor. Kwashiorkor is a native word which means "the sickness a child develops when another child is born." This is understandable because when another baby is born, the older one is deprived of the balanced protein in his mother's milk. Then, as often as not, he develops a bloated belly, edema, and brittle, orange-colored hair. Many children, deprived of balanced protein, also become mentally retarded or brain damaged.

At CIAT, the breeders began to direct their attention to improving the protein quality in corn. They crossed their new high-yielding hybrid with Opaque 2, a new plant sent down from Purdue University. This Opaque 2 seemed like the answer to everything because its white kernels were rich in balanced protein, in the form of lysine and tryptophan. The resulting hybrid, the New Opaque 2, was a plus for the poor who lived on corn and still more corn.

But, hungry or not, the Latin Americans didn't like the New Opaque 2. They didn't like the white color. They didn't like the mushy texture. They didn't like the taste.

To specialists trained in plant breeding, these objections posed no problems. In short order, they bred in a yellow color, a crisp texture, and a better taste, and developed a completely restructured plant. It had yellow kernels that were good looking, good tasting, and high yielding. It was, altogether, a supergrain, as rich in balanced protein as skimmed milk. And this corn carried no built-in starvation for the children of Latin America and parts of Asia and Africa. This corn, plus a few cents' worth of store-bought minerals and vitamins, was a nearly perfect food.

There is still a vexing problem. High-protein hybrids are not as productive as other hybrids. In the developing countries, where money is very scarce, productivity is important. Consequently, many farmers have been reluctant to plant the New Improved Opaque 2 hybrids. They prefer to plant for higher yields they can see, rather than for protein content they cannot see. Continued crossbreeding, however, has finally produced a newer Opaque 2 which promises to produce as well as the corn on the American prairies.

Other research specialists, at other international centers, working as genetic engineers, improved the drought-resistant millets and sorghums as well as some of the forage grasses. They even invented some plants. *Triticale* (known since 1888) was recently developed as a short, highly productive cereal grass. It is a cross between wheat and rye,

Improved grain sorghum being harvested by combine. *USDA–SCS photo*

and is more drought resistant and higher in protein than either of its parent plants.

The conquest of hunger became a green and glittering possibility in the early 1970's, when the restructured hybrids produced abundant harvests, right around the world. Wheat and rice, especially, topped all expectations, as yields increased by 50 percent, 100 percent, and in some instances by 1000 percent. India and the Philippines, long-time importers of rice, became exporters. Indeed, it was a green revolution, one which promised to overcome the population–food imbalance for all time.

That promise did not hold. The green revolution could

not be sustained without continued funds for miracle seeds, chemicals, suitable machines, irrigation systems, storage facilities, and roads to market. At the same time, deadly new plant viruses (immune to all known chemicals) appeared in the fields that had been planted to the new genetically controlled hybrids. Only a few of the low-yielding primitive grasses, which had not been eradicated from the fields, remained immune to those viruses. And so, global hunger once more became a grim possibility.

Again the plant breeders were challenged. They had developed their genetic skills so well, they could tailor plants according to specification. By drawing on the thousands of varieties stored in the seed banks, they could inbreed and crossbreed till they produced hybrids that were taller or shorter, that grew fewer leaves and heavier seed heads, that were responsive to fertilizer and resistant to drought or cold or plant diseases. They could produce hybrids that yielded abundantly and matured rapidly. They could produce hybrids that were rich in balanced protein, tasty, and attractive. And still—it was not enough to feed the world, whose population continued to increase while available cropland continued to shrink, as more and more acreage was withdrawn for urban needs and super highways.

The challenge—could the breeders produce even more productive cereal grasses, on less land and at less cost?

Knowing that beyond a certain point, the cereal grasses do not respond to increased applications of fertilizer or to improved technology, the specialists began looking in another direction. They began thinking in terms of creating more efficient do-it-yourself plants. But first they needed to solve two problems:

Their first problem concerned nitrogen: Could they stimulate the cereal grasses to produce their own nitrogen fertilizer and thereby reduce the need for expensive, commercial fertilizer? Could they make those grasses extract the nitrogen from the air which circulates around their roots?

Already, work in this area is proceeding at the University of Florida and attracting considerable attention. There, a group of researchers is trying to transfer the nitrogen-fix-

MORE MOUTHS WILL HAVE TO BE FED FROM SHRINKING LAND

average size of farm family 6.

1962

Each farm family fed 2.7 persons in addition to itself.

2.9 HECTARES

1975

Each farm family will have to feed 3.5 persons in addition to itself.

2.3 HECTARES

1985

Each farm family will have to feed 4.1 persons in addition to itself.

2.0 HECTARES

arable land per farm family

ing bacteria to the roots of an African forage grass. In other laboratories, researchers are working with the wild, recently discovered Brazilian grasses (including a tropical corn strain) that already fix their own nitrogen, but thrive only in very warm soils.

The second problem was concerned with food value: Could they stimulate the cereal grasses to increase the protein and carbohydrate content of their leaves and seeds? This question zeroes in on the photosynthetic efficiency of the green leaves which, in most instances, absorb only a fraction of the light energy that is available, and retain only about half of the CO_2 that is absorbed. If the photosynthetic process could be made more efficient in its use of light energy and CO_2, grass plants would be able to store more food.

The frontiers of science are vast, and the new biological technologies stretch from proposed grain farms in space to the more readily constructed "plastic farms" on earth, where the cereal grasses may be grown under plastic in controlled environments. But these are long-range proposals and their implementation is still far in the future.

• For the hungry of today, there's a short-range program that can immediately and dramatically increase the amount of grain that's available for human consumption. This is the *global housekeeping program*, which needs to be tackled from a number of directions.

Good global housekeeping is ecological housekeeping, designed to safeguard the harvests. This means that cereal crops, planted for man's use, should be consumed by man and not by his natural competitors. A certain amount of grain will normally be diverted into the stomachs of local birds and other wild animals. But consider the rodents. In one year, one rat eats as much grain as one egg-laying chicken. In one year, rodents damage, infect, and otherwise destroy one third of all the planted crops in the world.

In this, the last quarter of the twentieth century, the rat population has proliferated to an all-time high. Chemicals, used to boost grain production, have destroyed many biological enemies of the rat—owls, hawks, and snakes. This is ecological interference. It is not good ecological housekeeping.

Ecological housekeeping is also needed along many of the coastal areas that have been urbanized. With the areas urbanized, the natural feeding grounds for the birds have been destroyed, so vast, migrating flocks sweep inland to the grainfields and sometimes cut the standing harvests in half.

Another way to improve ecological housekeeping is to prevent the daily pile-up of thousands of tons of manure in the feedlots of some of the beef-producing countries. Through seepage, this manure contaminates the waterways. Recycling these wastes on a commercial scale would prevent this situation and would, at the same time, conserve high-level organic fertilizer for the grainfields.

There is also *technological housekeeping*, which refers to

the safeguarding of grain while it is in transit or storage. Currently, a good percentage of the harvested grain is lost (to assorted insects and other small creatures) between the field and the cooking pot. Another good percentage is lost through spoilage, because the harvest is often left in makeshift storage bins that are damp and moldy. And still more is sometimes left on the fields, where the farmers may live as much as ten miles from the nearest road. During the green revolution in India, when much was planted and much was raised, much was also never removed from the fields. Many farmers had no way of getting their huge harvests to market, and no place to store them, either. In one province, this problem was solved at the expense of the children. The harvests were locked inside the school buildings, and the children were locked out.

The technology is available to prevent spoilage, to build roads, and to construct storage depots. But the solution? The solution seems to lie in the political arena, but the minute the word "politics" is mentioned, a blizzard of plans, intended to conquer hunger, is loosed. These plans range from personalized moral restraint to strong world govern-

Improved grain storage facility in Bogota, Colombia.   *United Nations photo*

Modern steel silos in Turkey.　　　*Courtesy Toprak Mahsulleri Ofisi, Ankara*

ments, using even stronger dicta and backing them up with force. Certainly, the answer lies in planning, but these need to be realistic plans. They need to take cognizance of the galloping population, of the finite planet, and of the impact of mindless agricultural expansion on the environment. These plans need to be so designed that the grain which is needed is grown where it is needed, by the people who need it, and not by some strangers five thousand miles across the sea.

Such plans, implemented with technology that is adapted to given areas, might be designed to control the situation. Otherwise, as one eminent scientist put it, "If the situation isn't controlled by design, it will soon be controlled by disaster."

CHAPTER 13

The Grasses: Not Only for Food

A new multi-million dollar grass industry has been moving up front in the affluent countries, but it's an industry that produces neither cereal grain nor forage. It's the booming twentieth-century turf industry—producing turf for golf courses, racetracks, and parks, for highway embankments, private lawns, and institutional grounds, for military bases and memorial cemeteries.

Turf is a sod of soil with intertangled roots of creeping grasses. Under natural field conditions, these roots and these grasses form a dense carpet. Under professional care, new grasses, selected for wear resistance, form a turf so tough, it's practically child-proof. That's why you rarely see "Keep Off the Grass" signs anymore.

A hundred or more years ago, Americans would have laughed at the idea of a turf industry. Turf just naturally covered the land. Didn't the Indians streak across the plains, on foot or horseback, chasing a buckskin ball in a game that was later called lacrosse? Wasn't there more than enough turf for grazing cattle and sheep? Wasn't it available for building homestead shelters? Sod, cut with sharp-edged spades, made snug "soddies." Blocks of sod formed the walls, and strips of sod covered the roofs. Soddies warmed those old-timers in winter and cooled them in summer, even if they did get a bit muddy inside when it rained. Airports? There were plenty of grassy fields to serve those early, lightweight flying machines. As for cemetery turf, didn't many settlers have their own private burying grounds tucked away in a quiet green corner of the property?

Turf wasn't anything to think about. It was there. It was plentiful. And it renewed itself abundantly. Imagine the surprise, then, when the federal government became interested in the subject of turf. Under the Agricultural Appropriations Act (which was concerned mainly with reclaiming overstocked ranges and washed-out lands) the Congress, in 1901, actually allocated money for "determining . . . the best native and foreign [grass] species . . . for turfing lawns and pleasure grounds." The allocation? A modest $17,000.

The deliberate growing of turf, on a commercial scale, had to wait until the country became more urbanized. People who were crowded into concrete cities began hankering for greenery. Suddenly, or so it seemed, turf stopped being second cousin to the corn patch. If people wanted turf for beautification and recreation and safety along the highways, they had to buy it, and good turf wasn't all that plentiful anymore.

The first big step in the development of the turf industry was taken in 1920, when the Greens Section of the United States Golf Association lobbied vigorously, won the support of the USDA, and cooperatively engaged in a program of research. In short order, the program was expanded. Plant explorers set off to faraway lands to hunt for grasses suitable for putting greens and fairways, for shady lawns and semiarid localities. Researchers developed experimental plots. Here, they bred and inbred and crossbred, looking for grasses that would make the smoothest turf, grasses that were more wear- and drought- and disease-resistant, grasses that were more uniform in color. And right behind the Americans were the British. Traditionally

A section of bent-grass sod, whose fine texture is ideal for the golf course.
The Lawn Institute

interested in fine lawns and playing fields, the colonial-minded British established Turf Research Centers around the world—from Yorkshire, England, to New Zealand, New South Wales, Queensland, and Victoria in Australia, and to Capetown, South Africa.

One by one, the newly developed and imported turf grasses began to be listed in the seed catalogs. At first the listings were few. An early Burpee catalogue advertized fewer than a dozen varieties, half of them English-style

Majestic bluegrass—a lawn favorite.   *The Lawn Institute*

bluegrass. By the last quarter of the century, the ten largest seed companies listed something like three hundred varieties. These included the bent grasses, much loved by golfers who want velvety putting greens. These also included five warm-weather grasses—zoysia and centipede grasses from China, St. Augustine and carpet grasses from the West Indies, and Bermuda grass from Africa.

Understandably, these became popular in the southern states, but they have one drawback. They go dormant at

A natural bluegrass field in Kentucky, where seed was long gathered in this fashion each June. Most bluegrass seed is today agriculturally cropped rather than taken from natural stands such as this. *The Lawn Institute*

the first touch of frost and turn brown. (To counter this, some homeowners spray their lawns with green dye in the fall. Others, more ecology minded, overseed the area with cool-climate, quick germinating rye grass and enjoy a living lawn during the winter months.)

In most areas, well-cared-for turf is composed of a mix of new, improved, and imported grasses plus a number of the native meadow grasses, cut short. The most favored varieties in any region are those which are best adapted to the climate of that region.

In the United States and Canada and some of the other Western countries, turf production was boosted into the million-dollar bracket with the development of technologies that can produce lawns either in a few hours, or a couple of months, or a year at most. Gone are the days when

CLIMATIC REGIONS, IN WHICH THE FOLLOWING GRASSES ARE SUITABLE FOR LAWNS:

1. Kentucky bluegrass, red fescue and colonial bent grass. Tall fescue, bermuda and zoysia grasses in the southern part.

2. Bermuda and zoysia grasses. Centipede, carpet, and St. Augustine grasses in the southern part; tall fescue and Kentucky bluegrass in some northern areas.

3. St. Augustine, bermuda, zoysia, carpet, and bahia grasses.

4. Nonirrigated areas: crested wheat, buffalo, and blue grama grasses. Irrigated areas: Kentucky bluegrass and red fescue.

5. Nonirrigated areas: crested wheatgrass. Irrigated areas: Kentucky bluegrass and red fescue.

6. Colonial bent, Kentucky bluegrass, and red fescue.

English gardeners attributed the excellence of their lawns to the fact that they had been pampered for three hundred years. In line with today's speedy tempo, turf professionals can produce a near-perfect lawn between sunrise and sunset, by *sodding.*

Laden with rolls of sod that have been grown and machine-cut at the nursery, the trucks pull up to the site. The gardeners leap out and begin shouting orders as they prepare the soil bed. If the area is large, they plow it, disk-harrow it, and roll it firm with power equipment. If the area is small, it's prepared in much the same way with hand tools—spades and pitchforks and push rollers. After that, the sod is unrolled, laid on the soil bed, tamped down, top dressed, and watered. And there's the lawn, the greensward, the park (and the bill, of course). It's an in-

For an instant lawn, sod is harvested where it is grown, rolled, and then transported to a prepared soil bed elsewhere. *USDA–SCS photo*

stant lawn, and it looks for all the world like its famed English counterpart.

Slower than the sodded lawn but speedy, nevertheless, are lawns which are produced vegetatively, with stolons and plugs. Broadcast over the soil bed, or planted in narrow rows, the stolons root, spread, and form an unbroken turf in a couple of months. Plugs (pieces of sod about three inches in diameter), set into the bed at twelve-inch intervals, are equally effective.

Slowest of all the speedy lawns are the seeded ones, which may take up to a year to produce a well-established turf.

It has been estimated that, foot for foot, (when you count turf chemicals, tools, technology, and maintenance) professionally cultivated turf costs much more than the most carefully cultivated stand of corn, rice, or sugarcane. To cut down on this expense and the endless maintenance, an experimental idea is being proposed by some seed companies and some local offices of the Soil Conservation Service. This idea is the *ecological lawn*. It is recommended for the wide-open spaces where rainfall is scanty and irrigation water limited. It is recommended for large-scale subdivision building sites that have been bulldozed down to the clay.

An ecological lawn is an idea borrowed from nature. For milennia, thousands of acres of American "lawn" thrived

Ecological lawn, an experimental project undertaken in Kansas. Seen here in the center section of the picture, it is seeded to buffalo grass and bordered by blocks of bluestem.   *USDA–SCS photo, Manhattan, Kansas*

in the drier regions of the United States. Four native grasses, with roots and runners all tangled together, built this
sod. These were the buffalo grass, which grows short,
crisp, and curly; the fine-textured blue grama grass; the
side oats grama, which makes a field feel like a Persian carpet; and the little bluestem. The little bluestem, however,
is not considered suitable for the ecological lawn because it
grows too tall.

An ecological lawn is a lazy man's dream because, once
planted, these grasses grow mightily. They require no
watering, no fertilizing, and no more than two or three
mowings a year. But—they do require patience, because
they cannot be enjoyed until the second year after planting. That's because these staunch native grasses spend
the first year growing *downward* and developing a
good strong root system.

Anyone planning to lay down a lawn naturally thinks of
the runner grasses because they produce such good turf.
There is one grass, however, that nobody would select for
turf building. Although this grass sends out strong rhizomes from which new stems grow, it does not produce
turf. Instead, it produces a forest of woody stems that sway
and creak in the wind. This is the bamboo, a grass in the
genus *Bambusa*.

Bamboos come in all sizes and are native to all continents
except Europe. In the Far East, many grow unusually tall.
The *Dendrocalamus giganteus* of Ceylon grows taller than a
ten-story building. Others grow very fast, as much as three
feet in a single day. And still others, like the timber bamboo of southeast Asia, stretch up to their full height of seventy feet in six weeks.

In the highlands of Ecuador and Peru, there are climbing
bamboos, which clamber up tall plants and hang down like
green vines. In the southwestern United States, the *Sasa
pumila*, which is only a few inches tall, often serves as a
ground cover and sometimes even substitutes for turf. And
along the swampy Gulf Coast, there are still remnants of
bamboo groves, called canebrakes, which used to be so
thick that they served as hiding places for runaway slaves.

Bamboos may look slight alongside the palms, but some are 6 to 8 inches in diameter.
Courtesy IRRI, Philippines

Regardless of their size, the bamboos share certain characteristics. Their woody stems are hollow and covered with a shiny, waxlike surface. All stems are rigid. All are girdled with heavy nodes. All produce graceful, feathery leaves and are very strong. A study, conducted at the University of Puerto Rico, found that the tensile strength of *Bambusa tulda* is 60,000 pounds to the square inch.

In the Orient, the bamboo has long been the all-purpose grass that provides the natives with many of the necessities of life. The people may live in bamboo houses and send their children to bamboo school buildings. They may sit on bamboo mats, sleep on bamboo sheets as soft as silk, and use bamboo dishes. Wearing cone-shaped hats and in some instances coats and trousers made of bamboo, farmers use bamboo tools to till their little gardens, which are secured by bamboo fences. Later, they may transport their harvests to market in bamboo boxes and baskets and carts, over bamboo bridges that are sometimes suspended from tough bamboo cables.

Commercially, products made from bamboo form a good part of the Eastern export trade. Additionally, it provides China, India, Trinidad, and other countries with the pulp they need for making paper—a commodity in great demand by schools, newspapers, and publishing houses.

In the Western world, the demand for paper for publishing, record keeping, wrapping, tissues, and even baby diapers, is insatiable. It is also worrisome, because pulp is in short supply here, since so many slow-growing forests have been cut down. Considerable interest, consequently, is being shown in the research and development of certain bamboo forests, which produce a great deal of cellulose, grow quickly, and are therefore a speedy renewable resource.

As the century draws to a close, the spotlight focuses more and more brightly on the grasses as they affect our life and our lifestyle. In our urban society, turf is the green link between people and nature. In our industrial society, other grasses serve as the connecting link among the farm, the food bin, and the factory.

Strange as it may sound, our industrial society would suffer a slowdown were it not for the grasses. There is hardly one single thing that you touch every day that hasn't been manufactured, in part, with the aid of a grass product or a bit of grass waste.

The briquettes, for example, that you fire for your cookout are held together with a binder that is a by-product of corn, a cereal grass. The soap you wash with was probably made with crude corn oil. The leather wallet you carry?

Corn starch was used in the tanning process. Your brightly printed sport shirts, beach togs, bedsheets, and curtains? Starch and gum, derived from corn, carried the dyes that fixed those prints. Even the steepwater, left over from the corn-soaking cycle, is used to grow molds that produce penicillin and other antibiotics.

At many factories, waste products of grass become valuable commodities. Hulls from rice and oat seeds, as well as corncobs, are converted into huge tanks of *furfural*, an oily liquid that's useful in making many plastics, bleaching agents, insecticides and disinfectants, synthetic rubber, shoe dyes and paint removers. Wheat straw is turned into modern beehives, chair seats, and string. Perfume, by the barrel, is manufactured from lemon grass and ginger grass and citronella grass. And tons of cardboard and pasteboard are manufactured from the stems of wheat, rye, barley, and oats.

Aided by twentieth-century technology, grass for turf, just like grass for food and industrial uses, has become big business. In the final analysis, however, the continued success of this business depends on a balanced grass ecology—an ecology of water and temperature and hours of sunlight, of suitable soil that's stable, and a groundwater table that is uncontaminated by chemical salts and poisonous pollutants.

CHAPTER 14
Grass for the Human Spirit

Grass plants need one kind of ecology for growth. People need another kind for the human spirit.

The human body needs bread and meat. The human spirit needs green and open spaces. In our man-made culture, air pollutants darken the light of the sun; blinking signs and floodlights pierce the softness of night; and screeching sirens batter the ears. Assaulted by the stink of automobile exhaust, and surrounded by concrete, asphalt, and brick, the human spirit withers. It needs the green beauty of open spaces. It needs privacy and revitalization.

Green spaces, open to the sky, carpeted with grass and other growing plants, serve the "green" needs of our urban population. These green spaces are more than parks and playing fields and sodded traffic islands. They are greenbelts and wilderness areas and wildlife refuges and more.

Who hasn't dreamed of a little house in suburbia with a smooth, green lawn edged with ornamental grasses, bushes, and trees? For those who can afford it, a smooth, green lawn is also a status symbol. It proclaims the owners to be people of substance. Millennia past, the early farmer

A quiet pasture in New Zealand.   *Courtesy New Zealand Journal of Agriculture*

on the plains of Mesopotamia was similarly regarded as a man of substance if he had a circle of green grass near his living quarters. At that time, it was his sheep, tethered to the trees, that cropped the grass that produced the lawn. If a man owned many sheep, he soon acquired a number of such circular lawns and so established his worth. Then, even as now, children played on the grass and danced and raced and chased each other.

Perhaps the first lawns, planned for the human spirit, were those planted in China, in the first century B.C. There, 30,000 slaves cared for the vast lawns and pleasure gardens of Emperor Wu Ti. The lawn designs were simple, the grassy plots quiet, and the ornamental plantings artistically understated.

Sometime later, in the kingdom of Persia, royal gardens were laid out that were so tranquil and serene by day and so luminous by night that they were transcribed onto silken rugs and wall hangings. In the eleventh century, the Crusaders, returning from the Near Eastern wars, brought some of those silken rugs and hangings back to England.

Intrigued by the silken Persian greenery, the English kings and nobles were not long in creating their own gardens, English style. At first, these were merely green plots inside the castle walls, for the lords and ladies to dance on. Centuries later, these plots were replaced outside the walls by green playing fields for bowling and cricket. By the eighteenth century, great sweeping lawns became fashionable, the size of the lawn being indicative of the owner's wealth. For the nobility and the rich this was no problem because labor was cheap and plentiful. At about the same time as the Empire became a world power, English lawns, like the English flag, were planted at the colonial outposts by the military stationed there. And wherever the climate was cool and moist enough for bluegrass, those lawns flourished.

Also, in the eighteenth century, interior lawns and patios became part of the middle-class home in Spain and Portugal. In the United States, however, with free land available, lawns, like the other abundant natural resources, became part of the common man's heritage.

American settlers, in the main, had little time and little need for planted lawns. Surrounded by endless greenery and busy with building a new country, they were satisfied with village greens and used them as communal gathering places. These greens were open squares, bordered by church and school, homes and shops. Here, the sheep grazed. Here, the children romped. Here, their elders bowled and pitched horseshoes after the day's work was done. Later, as the country grew richer and leisure time became available among the well-to-do, green spaces with good turf were set aside for horse racing, golf, and tennis. Indeed, "turf" has come to be synonymous today with "horse racing."

Currently, in small towns as well as in high-rise cities, a

green, turfed space is a safe playground for children. It is a quiet retreat for adults. It is a flood-control factor in conservation. Urban lawns, reduced to pocket-handker-chief size, nevertheless act as blotters when it rains. As the raindrops slide down the grass leaves and stems, they are caught by the grass roots and held in the matted earth below.

To retain the beauty of the countryside and to prevent mud floods, Los Angeles, with its steeply sloped hinter-land, has adopted a Green Hills Law, which is being eyed by other cities. This law, in an attempt to control hillside erosion, requires contractors to plant and maintain a grass cover on any slopes or cuts created by them during construction.

Sometimes lawns, miniature golf courses, and bowling greens are covered with *plastic grass*—polystyrene turf and plasta strips. This artificial grass looks beautiful, just like the real thing, but there the similarity ends. Plastic turf cannot absorb the falling rain. The runoff gouges the soil around edgings and plantings. It creates mud-floods. It chokes storm sewers.

On children's playgrounds or football stadiums, plastic grass creates another kind of ecological disaster. Along with shedding rainwater, the plastic fibers fail to biodegrade dust, dirt, sputum, and the deposits of dogs and cats, decaying insects and worms. A sanitation problem is thus created, and for a player, a scraped knee may become an infected knee.

Sometimes plastic turf, cement playgrounds, asphalt driveways or flagged patios are painted to resemble grass. These inert materials halt the interaction of air and soil, water and sunlight, which keeps the ecosystem in balance. They are no substitutes for the green and growing grass.

In open spaces, grass provides quiet ecological pluses for the human spirit. It freshens and cleanses the air. It re-duces glare and noise. It air-conditions the environment. It absorbs odors.

Take a walk in the park on a sunny day. Sit on the grass. Run on it. Roll on it. Breathe deeply. The air smells fresher, and it is fresher. The grass leaves, which are carrying on

Temperature study, showing the value of a good grass cover.   *USDA–SCS photo*

the process of photosynthesis, are taking in carbon dioxide and releasing oxygen, thereby diluting the contaminants in the city air. The green leaves are also *transpiring*, releasing water vapor into the air. On a sunny summer day, an acre of good turf may release as much as 7,000 gallons of water through transpiration and evaporation. In addition, grass absorbs heat. In a study conducted at Michigan State University, the thermometer recorded a surface temperature of 163 degrees Fahrenheit on the artificial turf of the stadium, but only 88 degrees on the grass adjoining the stadium. In another study, the temperature of a bare field rose to 114 degrees, but the surface temperature of a grass plot, just six feet away, remained at 84 degrees. And even greater differences exist between grass surfaces and man-made surfaces such as sidewalks and brick walls.

Grass leaves retain and disperse water during a rainstorm.   *USDA–SCS photo*

Now take a ride on a superhighway. When the road runs between tall buildings or high retaining walls, the noise is unnerving, the dust often visible. But wait till the road winds between sloping, grass-covered highway embankments. Then the noise dies away, the dust settles, and if it's summer time, the temperature drops noticeably.

The noise dies away because the grass leaves (as well as the leaves of other nearby plants) absorb many of the sound waves. On some well-sodded embankments, noise is reduced by as much as ten decibels. In a depressed freeway, with well-sodded banks, noise may be cut by 50 percent. And dust disappears because the leaves, being hairy and moist, trap the floating dust particles, the soot and smoke and pollen, as well as the sun's heat.

Of course, some of the invisible pollutants that the grasses absorb may injure them—turn them yellow or kill them altogether. As a matter of fact, long before people are aware of the danger, some grasses sound their early-warning sys-

Severe roadside erosion deposits tons of silt on road and creates driving hazards.
USDA–SCS photo

Roadside cut being stabilized.   *USDA–SCS photo*

For beautification and erosion control, seed and fertilizer are first applied to a highway embankment, then covered with a wood-fiber mulch.   *USDA–SCS photo*

A roadbank, sloped and seeded or sodded, reduces noise and traps dust.
USDA–SCS photo

tems. Red fescue and bent grass signal sulphur dioxide in the air. Bluegrass and bent grass signal ozone in the air.

The grasses that cover the earth provide us with our daily bread. "But man does not live by bread only. . . . " Bread sustains his body, but beauty sustains his spirit. Body and spirit, operating as one, are dependent on a balanced ecosystem. In turn, the ecosystem is dependent on grass.

But the grasses are at the mercy of man. Let him misuse them, and he creates a wasteland that starves his body and withers his spirit. Let him care for them, and he finds the grasses almost imperishable, almost everlasting, almost eternal, because grass is the benediction of nature.

Appendix

The Grasses

COMMON NAMES	SCIENTIFIC
Bahia grass	*Paspalum notatum*
Barley	*Hordeum vulgare*
Bent grass (creeping)	*Agrostis palustris*
Bermuda grass	*Cynodon dactylon*
Bluegrass (Kentucky)	*Poa pratensis*
Bluestem	
big	*Andropogon gerardii*
little	*Andropogon scoparius*
Bromegrass (smooth)	*Bromus inermis*
Buffalo grass	*Buchloæd actyloides*
Canary grass	*Phalaris canariensis*
Cordgrass (big)	*Spartina cynosuroides*
Corn: Indian corn; maize	*Zea mays*
Fescue	
red	*Festuca rubra*
tall	*Festuca arundinacea*
Guinea grass	*Panicum maximum*
Love grass	
weeping	*Eragrostis curvula*
Millet	*Setaria faberi*
(giant foxtail)	
Oats	*Avena sativa*
Orchard grass	*Dactylis glomerata*
Redtop	*Agrostis alba*
Ribbon grass	*Phalaris arundinacea*
Rice	*Oryza sativa*
Rye	*Secale cereale*
Side oats grama	*Bouteloua curtipendula*
Sorghum	*Sorghum bicolor (L.) Moench*
Sudan grass	*Sorghum bicolor (L.) Moench*
Sugarcane	*Saccharum officinarum*
Timothy	*Phleum pratense*
Triticale	*A hybrid of wheat and rye—no scientific name.*
Wheat	*Triticum aestivum*

Selected References

Archer, Sellers G., and Bunch, Clarence E., *The American Grass Book*. Norman, Okla.: University of Oklahoma Press, 1953.

Borgstrom, Georg, *Focal Points: A Global Food Strategy*. New York: Macmillan, 1973.

———*The Hungry Planet*. New York: Macmillan, 1972.

Brown, Lester R., and Eckholm, Erik, *By Bread Alone*. New York: Praeger Publishers, 1974.

Brown, Lester R., and Finsterbusch, Gail W., *Man and His Environment: Food*. New York: Harper and Row, 1972.

Carter, Vernon Gill, and Dale, Tom, *Topsoil and Civilization*. Norman, Okla: University of Oklahoma Press, 1974.

Crockett, James Underwood, and the Editors of Time-Life Books, *Lawns and Ground Covers*. New York: Time-Life Books, 1971.

Freeman, Orville L., *World Without Hunger*. New York: Frederick A. Praeger, 1968.

Hallacy, D. S., *The Geometry of Hunger*. New York: Harper and Row, 1972.

Heady, Eleanor B., *Coat of the Earth*. New York: W. W. Norton and Co., 1968.

Moore, A. C., *The Grasses*. New York: Macmillan, 1960.

Naden, Corinne J., *Grasslands Around the World*. NNew York: Franklin Watts, 1970.

Riedman, Sarah R., *Grass, Our Greatest Crop*. New York: Thomas Nelson and Sons, 1952.

Staten, H. W., *Grasses and Grassland Farming*. New York: Devon-Adair Co., 1952.

Udall, Stewart L., *The Quiet Crisis*. New York: Holt, Rinehart and Winston, 1963.

FAO Publications

International Research in Agriculture by the Consultative Group on International Agricultural Research (co-sponsored by the FAO, the U.N. Development Programme and the World Bank), New York, Consultative Group on International Agriculture, 1974.

A Strategy for Plenty. FAO of the United Nations. New York: FAO, 1970.

Whyte, R. O., and Moir, T. R. G., and Cooper, J. P., *Grasses in Agriculture*. Rome: FAO, 1965.

Rockefeller Foundation Publications

R. F. Illustrated for 1973, 1974, 1975. New York.
Strategy for the Conquest of Hunger. Proceedings of a symposium convened by the Rockefeller Foundation, 1968.

USDA Publications. U.S. Government Printing Office, Washington, D.C.

Conquest of the Land through 7,000 Years. USDA Agriculture Information Bulletin No. 99.
Early American Soil Conservationists. USDA Miscellaneous Publication No. 449.
Grass. USDA Yearbook of Agriculture for 1948.
Grass in Conservation in the U.S. USDA SCS-TP-143, 1964.
Grasses and Legumes for Soil Conservation in the Pacific Northwest and Great Basin States. USDA Agriculture Handbook No. 339.
Landscape for Living, USDA Yearbook of Agriculture for 1972.
100 Native Forage Grasses in Eleven Southern States. USDA Handbook No. 389.
Soil Conservation at Home: Tips for City and Suburban Dwellers. USDA-AB 244.
The Soil that Went to Town, USDA A1B95.

Index